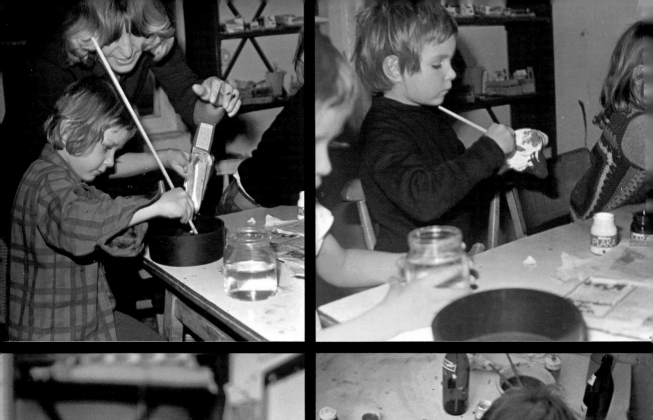

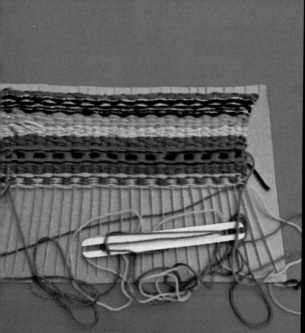

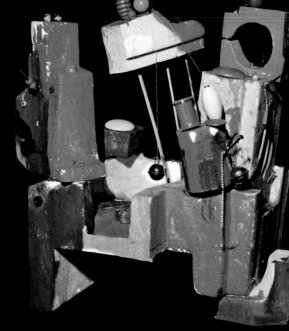

THE REINHOLD BOOK OF ART AND CRAFT TECHNIQUES

THE REINHOLD BOOK OF ART AND CRAFT TECHNIQUES

for parents, teachers, and children

VNR VAN NOSTRAND REINHOLD COMPANY
New York Cincinnati Toronto London Melbourne

Copyright © 1976 by Litton Educational Publishing, Inc.
Translation from the German by Alba Lorman
This book was originally published in Germany in ten
separate volumes under the series title *Basteln mit Kindern*.
Copyright © 1973, 1974 and 1975 by Otto Maier Verlag,
Ravensburg, Germany.

Library of Congress Catalog Card Number 75-38619
ISBN 0-442-26876-9 (paper)
ISBN 0-442-26875-0 (cloth)

Printed in the United States of America.

Published in 1976 by Van Nostrand Reinhold Company
a division of Litton Education Publishing, Inc.
450 West 33rd Street, New York, NY 10001

Van Nostrand Reinhold Limited
1410 Birchmount Road, Scarborough, Ontario   M1P 2E7,
Canada

Van Nostrand Reinhold Australia Pty. Limited
17 Queen Street, Mitcham, Victoria 3132, Australia

Van Nostrand Reinhold Company Limited
Molly Millars Lane, Wokingham, Berkshire, England

16 15 14 13 12 11 10 9 8 7 6 5 4 3 2 1

Library of Congress Cataloging in Publication Data
Main entry under title:

The Reinhold book of art and craft techniques .

  Translation of Basteln mit Kindern.
  Includes index.
  1. Handicraft—Study and teaching.
TT157.B3513   745.5   75-38619
ISBN 0-442-26876-9 pbk.
ISBN 0-442-26875-0

CONTENTS

INTRODUCTION

This volume is for parents, teachers, and social workers who work with children between the ages of three and eight. While the basic idea of the book is that children should be occupied playfully with a hobby, it is also important that adults gain information on how to present techniques and materials to children according to their age level and skill. Children like to work on their own as much as possible, so adult interference should be kept to the absolute minimum. Every educator knows that nothing will limit a child's imagination and creativity more than excessive competition and pressure for achievement. The joys of handling the materials and determining their possibilities are more important than the finished product. Each single step of a project presents an important experience for a child in expressing his own desires and capabilities.

1. PAPER-AND-PASTE ANIMALS

by Günter Grieshaber

Not every child will discover on his own that one can shape a figure or an animal of papier-mâché. Demonstration, therefore, is an important first step, because children become bored by modeling the same unchallenging blobs all the time. The child's creativity and feeling for materials and their design possibilities should be developed. Thus the information presented here for the adult is mostly relative to the materials, since knowledge about processing and especially preparation of the materials provides the groundwork for success. By working with clay, rocks, wood, paper, paste, etc., the child becomes familiar with these media and gets to know the structures of various shapes by creating the objects. Moreover, his powers of observation and the flexibility of his hands are being trained, and his imagination is stimulated by shaping the various materials.

If you live and work with children, you know how quickly they become tired of one thing and want to move on to new activities and games. Considering the quality and size of the animals, the time required to make them is short. Working on other materials, such as wood or clay, would take much longer. Paper-and-paste animals have

another advantage: they are not ready right away and have to dry, so the child can work in intervals of twenty minutes to one hour, according to his perseverance.

Materials Needed

Newspaper; wallpaper paste and a suitable container; left-over white wall paint (in spray form); paintbox of watercolors or other colors soluble in water (tempera, dispersion paint, or distemper); bristle brushes 3/16", 3/8", and 7/8" wide.

Preparation of Working Materials

The table in the nursery, basement, playroom, or garden should be about twenty inches high for children two to three years old, and twenty-three inches high for children four to six years old. Children of seven can work on regular tables, between twenty-seven and twenty-nine inches high. Each child should have at least one square yard of working space. Cover the table with a large piece of cardboard. Children prefer to stand during sculpting and painting, but chairs should be placed nearby for resting. The easiest materials to work with are inferior-grade papers, such as newspaper. Stiff paper, such as that used in some art magazines, is unsuitable.

You can buy wallpaper paste in paint stores, hardware stores, hobby stores, or toy departments in department stores. A five-ounce package is ample. Mix powder and water as directed on the package, but do not mix the entire package unless you want to make several large animals. Half the package is sufficient for a start. The container for the paste should be large enough for children to dip their hands in. When you are working with several children, wide, flat containers are best, such as old cake tins, lids of cookie boxes, etc. Wallpaper paste is neither poisonous nor harmful to the hands, but the children should not get it into their eyes, since it might cause a slight burning.

For the use of colors, see the instructions at the end of this chapter.

9

The Basic Shape Looks Like an Egg

Regardless of the child's age, it is best not to determine beforehand what animal or creature should be made. A child rarely creates by imagination; he starts to handle the material and is inspired during the working process. First make a simple basic shape, similar to an egg. If the child wants to start off right away with another basic shape, leave him alone. The goal is a fully three-dimensional form.

Newspaper should be opened
up and crumpled into a loose ball
with both hands. This should be
repeated with more sheets of
newspaper, perhaps five or ten,
depending on the size of the
basic shape.

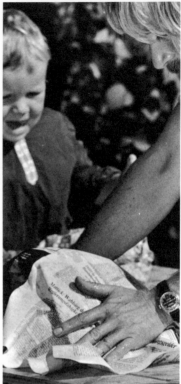

Now the upper side of the heap of paper balls is covered with a sheet of newspaper that has been thickly covered with paste on one side by hand or brush. This "skin" is pressed down on the top and sides. More layers of paper are added immediately, so that the paper skin becomes thicker and firmer and it is less likely to tear. After the entire form is turned over carefully, the same procedure is followed on the other side.

Now small pieces of paper are pasted around the basic form in order to smooth out the many crevices and uneven parts. Larger pieces of paper may be used on larger forms. On small and strongly arched shapes, only small pieces of paper will create a tight bond without creasing. Finally, a thin layer of paste should be applied all over so that the paper does not flake off when the form is drying. In summer the form will dry in the sun within a few hours. Air drying will take several days. In winter the drying time may be shortened by placing the form close to a radiator—or use a hair dryer. As soon as a hard skin has formed, work can continue. If the first step is completed and the child still wants to go on, more large and small basic forms may be made. Since small children will still find it difficult to keep the balls together when making the basic form, the adult should help with this stage.

of working is just right for the two- to-six-year-old child, do not interfere. For example, a child will shape balls of paper and paste in quick succession in various sizes and arrange them according to size: this is going to be a snake. Now you should help the child press the balls against each other and cover them with paste skin. The best way to make a skin for a snake is to use strips of paper, so that the structure does not fall apart.

In the course of shaping the balls, the children should keep dipping both hands in the paste so that the entire surface of the balls becomes sticky and they adhere to each other. Now the heap of balls will no longer fall apart and the children can apply paper skins on their own, with grown-ups helping only when needed.

If the child is left alone, he frequently starts to make a small form out of a single ball and paste and afterward identifies it as a particular animal. However, the longer the child kneads and crumples the material— which in itself is great fun— the more it changes from paper and paste to papier-mâché. The resulting animal will no longer have the consistency of the lightweight filling of loose balls, thus making it easy to create larger forms. Since this way

fection will be boring for the child. The egg shape serves as a solid base for adding the necessary parts that character-ize the various animals. You may attach bristles for a hedge-hog, ears for rabbits, wings for penguins, a neck, head, eyes, mouth, fins, tail, legs, or feet with toes and claws.

For making the auxiliary parts of a fish, for instance, let the chil-dren prepare the same basic form as described earlier. Make a hole by pushing a knife, a scissors, or any other pointed tool in the back or side of the body, wherever the fins should be. This hole should be large enough to insert two or three fingers.

How to Make a Fish Out of the Basic Egg-Shaped Form

The basic egg-shaped form to be used for developing various animals dries in two to three days and weighs very little, due to the empty spaces inside. The single layers of paper adhere well to each other; in spite of the child's clumsy handling, they no longer fall apart. During drying the form may sag a little, but this can be corrected any time by adding more balls and paste. However, too much per-

Then the child should dip his hands in paste and crumple a piece of newspaper into a round or long fin shape. This should be enlarged with four or five more crumpled-up sheets. Then cover the balls with dry paper, forming a point on one side that fits in the prepared hole. The crumpled-up shapes may be pressed against the already sticky parts. The crumpled-up mass of paper should protrude from the basic form about the width of a hand, just like a fin.

Don't be surprised at unexpected results, such as enormous eyes or giant fins. If children want fins or other parts to stick out a great deal from the basic form, these should not be crumpled up but should be made by rolling up several sheets of newspaper. Such a roll is then folded in the middle and the bent part is pushed into the prepared hole of the basic egg form. Then the hole should be filled with paper balls dipped in paste, and the fins should be covered with paper until the desired shape is obtained. If the fins are too thin, the sheets of newspaper have to be folded to the desired width, and paste should be applied continuously, so that the layers of paper stick well to each other without any gaps. This, of course, will make the fins heavier. If they should bend too much, let them dry first before inserting and securing them in the holes.

Now the fins should be pasted tightly to the main body. This is done by attaching paper strips over fin and body, thus joining them together and forming a secure skin. If a smooth transition between fin and body is desired, stuff small balls of paper in the corners between the two parts and cover them with paper strips having paste on both sides. This also serves to secure any protruding parts. The child should decide the size and shape of the fins. Frequently children have completely different ideas from grown-ups about the significance of this or that accessory.

19

sired size by adding more paper. After drying, insert it in the body and secure it by covering it with more sticky paper strips.

Follow the same procedure to make a head and a neck. To make hedgehog quills and similar small shapes, put paste on smaller pieces of paper and press them into the desired shape. It is much harder to make papier-mâché animals with long, thin, and graceful legs, like birds, horses, or giraffes. Start by forming the bodies, and especially the legs, with wire and then proceed by attaching paper and paste to the wire frame.

Other Animals

Many animals may be developed from the basic egg shape. Best suited are animals with pronounced round shapes, like turtles, penguins, hedgehogs, hens, or fish. If the children are a little older and have gained more dexterity with paper and paste, they can attempt a hippopotamus, a rhinoceros, a beaver, an elephant, a pig, a walrus, or a sea lion. The thick legs of a rhinoceros or a hippopotamus or an elephant are made as follows: crumple the paper into a sausage shape and roll it tightly into a sheet of newspaper that has first been covered with paste. Then strike one end of the leg on the table until the foot broadens. The foot can now be enlarged to any de-

What Colors to Use and How to Handle Them

It is not necessary to buy new colors for painting the animals if a child already owns a good box of watercolors. Since watercolors are not opaque enough to cover the newsprint, the entire animal should be covered first with white dispersion or leftover wall paint. Once this paint is dry it does not mix with the watercolors and is a good primer for further painting. However, if water-soluble white paint from the box is used as a foundation, it will dissolve when it is painted over, and the white color will mix with the colors used on top of it. The colors will become milky and lose their luminosity (milky colors should only be used on purpose, not unintentionally).

Luminous and saturated hues can be obtained by adding water to the paper cups holding the colors and soaking them for five to ten minutes before use. Then a creamy color may be mixed with a brush, and the resulting effect is similar to tempera or poster colors. Children who own poster colors, of course, will have less trouble. They can apply the desired color without any primer and without lengthy mixing. Caution: poster colors are usually hard to get out of fabrics! Finger paints are less suitable for painting larger surfaces, but they are much better later on for stippling. It is very effective to apply thin and very wet watercolors quickly over the white primer coat and then to wipe them with a rag. The protruding parts will become almost white and the color will remain in the deeper crevices.

In order to make the finished animal more durable and stable, it can be covered with a colorless fixative. This has to be applied very sparingly, since a thick layer might easily appear milky. You can also spray the animal with lacquer, but this should only be done by an adult; it is too dangerous for children.

How to Paint Animals

As a rule children are so strongly stimulated by an open paint box and brushes that they want to start painting right away. The job might even be finished without the grown-up's interference. First a base color is chosen by the child and applied with a wide brush. If a child is somewhat timid and undecided, the grown-up may help by demonstrating how brush strokes or various color specks may be done.

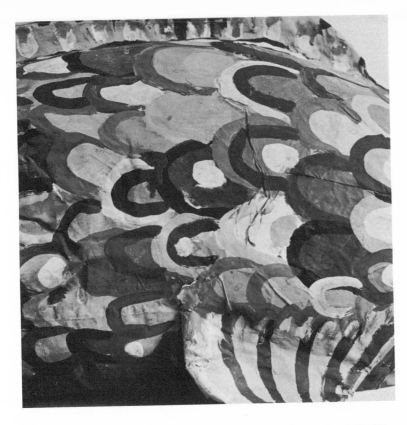

For instance, a fish has a covering of scales. One can explain that this fish skin is made up of many small parts and that these parts may shine in many colors. Many children will find out the structures of color and form by themselves and put small dots of color all over the colored foundation. In order to avoid too many colors, one may suggest the use of only one or two different colors, or that the head, fins, or tail (the smaller shapes) might be covered with small dots while the rest of the body is covered with larger ones. The child should be encouraged to find as many new lines and shapes as may be suited to the particular animal. By applying large dots of color or lines over larger areas and small dots on smaller parts of the animal, the contrast between large and small protruding parts may be emphasized.

When the eyes, ears, nose, mouth, feet, fins, and tail are painted, care should be taken that they appear to protrude properly out of the body and are not just attached. Both size and contrasting colors are important for the overall effect. Sometimes small eyes may appear more effective due to their strong color than large eyes without strong color contrasts or without clearly recognizable shapes.

Surface Treatments with Other Materials

If the child does not want to paint the animal, he may prefer to glue on various materials. If animals should appear hairy or shaggy, they may be covered with pieces of wool. One may also put drinking straws in rows next to each other, or glue on various types of paper cut into strips or torn up. Also, the use of solid or patterned fabric remnants may be intriguing. There are no limits to the imagination.

2. MASKS

by Günter Grieshaber

One of the most exciting games for children is transforming themselves into another character. That is why masks, offering an instant disguise, have a magic attraction for all children, whether they are outgoing or introverted. A child will spontaneously slip inside a fairy-tale animal or human figure, his imagination is stimulated, he links himself closely with his assumed role. Thus disguised and covered up, he loses a good deal of ineptitude and inhibition by creating his own world of reality and fiction. Here the adult is in for some surprises. If children are given a chance to design and make their own masks, they will simply overflow with ideas. After a few instructions this occupation can be carried out with groups of children as well as with one child.

In this chapter are four ways of producing masks:
—Cutting out paper bags
—Assembling and gluing boxes in various shapes and sizes
—Producing a basic hollow framework of strips of cardboard, on top of which the actual mask is molded by pasting down paper and papier-mâché.
—Shaping a solid body with paper balls or clay, on top of which the molding can be done

Materials Needed

Newspapers, brown wrapping paper, small and large paper bags, cardboard, boxes of various shapes and sizes, clay, scissors, a sharp knife, glue, paste, felt pens, poster colors, watercolors, brushes, string.

Working Conditions

A large table or the floor, covered with newspapers or brown wrapping paper, is best. Children like to cut, model, or paint standing up; therefore no chairs are needed. If the weather is good, work can be done outdoors, where cleaning up is somewhat easier.

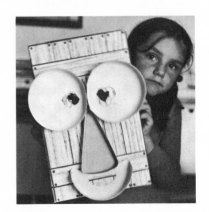

Masks Made of Small Paper Bags

You will need small bags or brown wrapping paper, glue, felt pens, scissors, crepe paper, colored papers, and other decorative materials. This kind of mask is easy to make, so it is suitable for very small children. The small bags may be bought, or made as follows: turn over a corner of a sheet of brown wrapping paper to form a double triangle, leaving a strip along one side for gluing. The child cuts out the triangle, folds over the extra strip, and glues it down. When making rectangular bags, the paper should be folded to the required size, with an extra strip added for gluing on both the long side and the short side.

Of course, the ready-made bags available at supermarkets may also be used. (Caution: do not use plastic bags, because they are too dangerous for children, who play with them and pull them over their heads before holes have been cut.) After the bag is made, the child pulls the

finished bag over his head and indicates the position of the eyes. This may be done by another child, who can mark the spots with a felt pen. Then the bag is taken off and the eyes are cut out. If the holes are first cut small, so that they can be opened up, eyelids can be made. If these flaps are cut with fringes, they even make funny lashes.

All kinds of pointed, angular, or round shapes may be cut in the bag, in a procedure similar to the folding and cutting of paper stars. What a surprise when the children discover that their cutouts and motifs come out doubled or changed when they open up the bags.

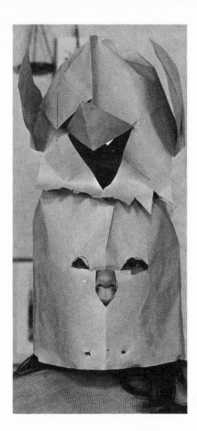

The possibilities are unlimited for cutting sections out of pointed bags, opening them up, gluing, and painting. A few of them should be demonstrated by an adult, and then the children should be encouraged to continue cutting and experimenting on their own.

Masks Made of Large Paper Bags

Large paper bags from a paper mill or building contractor provide simple but delightful possibilities for children to dress up from top to toe. Cut two large semicircles into the bag at shoulder height. When the bag is pulled over his head, the child may stick his arms through and wear the bag like a shirt. Bend over two corners of the bag so that they lie flat against the head and shoulders, and right away a hood has been created. Again eyes, nose, and mouth may be cut out. The original bag is no longer recognizable when gay strips of crepe paper are attached. If they are double-thickness bags, there are many more design possibilities. You can cut feathers, fins, or wings out of the two layers, or only one, as shown by the bird mask. If only the outer layer is cut from top to bottom, it becomes a coatlike wrap.

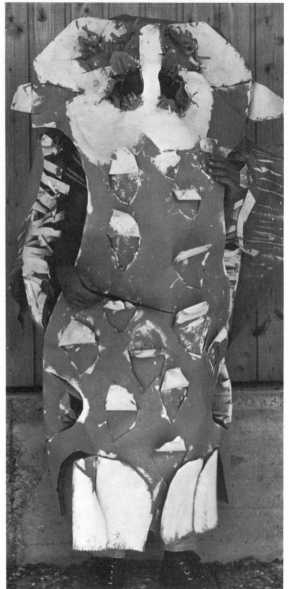

Masks Made of Boxes

Boxes available in any household may be used: shoe boxes, cheese containers, match boxes, and many more. Take a larger box as your base, maybe a shoe box. Cut out a semi-circle for the neck on one of the narrow sides so the mask can be adjusted to the child's face. Again, holes for the eyes are marked and cut out.

Then the children start to fashion the face of the mask with small boxes. Eyes, ears, nose, and mouth may be made from small round and square boxes.

For fastening the mask around the head, drill a hole in each side of the box near the back, insert a piece of string, and make a knot.

The mask may be decorated further with many colorful details. Here a boy has used wood shavings to make bushy curls and a beard. Everything is fastened with glue. A lively expression may also be achieved with bundles of straw, yarn, and fringes of fabric and paper.

**Masks Made on a Framework
of Cardboard Strips**

For the frame, cut a strip of flexible cardboard about twenty inches long, fit it closely round the face for size, and glue the ends together. Glue additional strips across the length and width to form a dome. Near the nose the strip may be bent to a point in order to leave enough room for the child's nose. When completed, the framework should look like one half of a giant egg.

Holes for eyes and mouth may be cut out easily with a pointed knife. If the nose, ears, and other features are not planned to be protruding, painting may start right away (see "Painting the masks"). If the children want to do some more work on the mask, they may continue to spread paste on strips of newspaper and shape the nose, chin, cheeks, ears, teeth, warts, or whatever they may think of. Every so often large pieces of newspaper covered with paste should be placed over the newly shaped protuberances to secure them firmly to the base.

With your hands, spread paste over sheets of newspaper and cover the framework with the paper. The more papers that are pasted down, the thicker and firmer the mask. Since it will now be very wet and could easily be damaged, the job of making the eyes and other details should wait until it is quite dry. The mask will take a few hours to dry in the sun, but only half an hour in the oven. It is good for the children to be occupied with other games in the meantime, before completing the job. The smaller the children, the less they will absorb several operations in one afternoon.

of paper may be crumpled up for the nose, which is attached and pasted over with straight pieces of paper. This basic form dries quickly. It may also be made firmer by wrapping some string around it. The basic form can also be made of clay, if it is available. Frequently children prefer the latter technique, since the rough outlines of a face may be made much more lifelike with clay.

At first, the children should touch and stroke their own faces to remind themselves of the most outstanding shapes, such as nose, chin, ears, and cheekbones. Then they shape a large body of clay and attach a long strip for the nose and round ones for the chin and eyes. Once the rough shape is finished, it may be dried in the sun or in a preheated oven. This provides a natural interruption of work. Obviously small children will not always understand the connection between molding the clay form and the later completion of the mask, due to this lapse of time. It is important, therefore, that they enjoy each step in the course of the project. When the mask is finally completed by following all the steps, all the phases of the project should be explained to the children so that they can understand the procedure. Before continuing to work on the clay

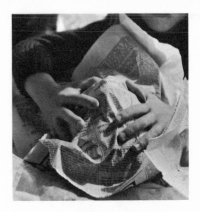

form, rub it with oil and cover it with a sheet of newspaper. This will facilitate lifting the mask later on.

How Masks are Shaped on a Paper or Clay Base

Since molded masks cannot be completed quickly, it is desirable to do them with children in more than one session. Tightly crumple up enough sheets of newspaper to make a form the size of a child's face; surround this framework with large pieces of paper covered with paste to hold it together. Additional balls

Now make layers of papers covered with paste and mold into shape, as with the crumpled-up paper method. Molding with papier-mâché is particularly attractive. If several masks are planned, it is best to prepare a whole bucket of papier-mâché. Proceed as follows: sheets of newspaper are mixed with paste, then shredded or torn in narrow strips. This is always a source of enjoyment for children. Then the strips are thrown into a bucket filled with about eight inches of water. Once the bucket is full of paper, the children may crumple it up and move it around until the paper is fully saturated.

Now shape small balls and tightly squeeze out the water. Take a small can of prepared paste and cover the balls with the contents. This makes a smooth mixture that can be used for molding. The surface of the finished form then may be further smoothed out.

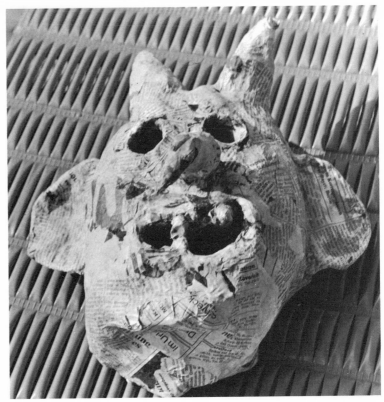

Very small children may not be able to shape the openings for the eyes or the mouth, or they may even forget them altogether. They should be made aware of this and assisted with the procedure. In order to improve the shaping of the eyes, for instance, rings may be cut out of a small cardboard roll (here it is the inside of a roll of toilet paper). These can be pressed onto the face, providing the outlines of the eyes, and they are then covered with papier-mâché.

On the whole, the adult should limit himself to giving advice and provide help only if absolutely necessary. (For instance, if a form falls apart, a few more layers of paste-covered paper strips should be added.) It is essential that the children become familiar with the materials and their design possibilities. This will stimulate and train the imagination and observation and provide experience in turning a rough shape into a form with fine lines, surfaces, and curves.

Finally, the still-moist mask is decorated by sticking into it and gluing on all kinds of small objects and waste products, in order to make it a very personal work: chicken or bird feathers, string, straw, matches, twigs, yarn, wood shavings, paper fringes, beads, bottle corks, matchboxes, rags, and various scraps of fabric. These materials may also be painted in many colors and tied into chains.

To fasten the mask to the head, make small holes on the sides and top of the mask with a pointed object; after it is dry, pull string or elastic through. If the mask is already dry, these holes can be made with an awl.

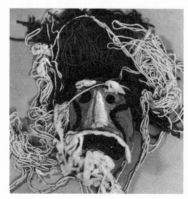

get quite dry after they are painted so that the soggy paper hardens again and the bright colors do not run.

All masks may be painted, although some will already look colorful and effective with their decorations, making painting unnecessary. If the surface of the mask is made of newspaper, it is best to use poster colors because of their opacity. Light, solid-colored areas may be painted with the usual watercolors.

Painting the Masks

You will need: a box of water-color paints or poster colors, a bristle brush about three-fourths-inch wide for large surfaces, smaller brushes, and several empty containers for mixing the colors and washing the brushes. The colors become more luminous and saturated by filling the containers with

water five to ten minutes before use and letting them soak. Finger paints are less suitable for painting large areas, but they are useful for later stippling. Children need no encouragement with paints; they are quite spontaneous in their use of both paints and brushes. It will take only a few minutes for their masks to become brightly colored. It is best to let the masks

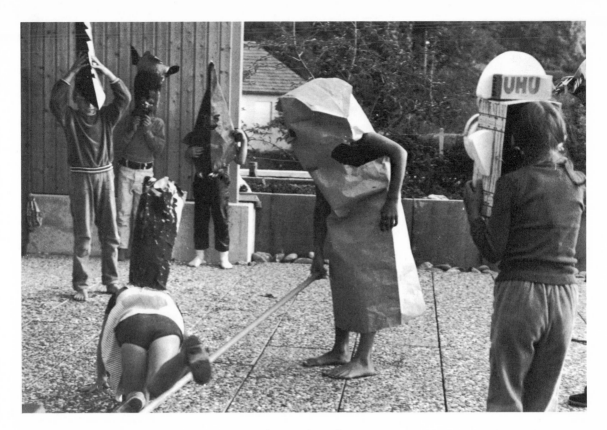

Then comes the great moment
when the children have completed their masks! For the
crowning glory you can arrange
a parade or a play so that each
child may show off his mask
or act out a role. Or they can
compose a dance; the familiar
children's rounds and guess-
ing games provide new excite-
ment when they are dressed
up in their own creations. Give
the children ample opportunity
to utilize the self-made masks
and make them part of their
games.

3. PUPPETS

by Irmgard Muenk

Puppets can be made by children of four and up; there is no upper age limit. Older children never regard puppets, like so many other hobbies, as "baby toys." Children of any age can "use" puppets and each will turn out entirely different according to its maker. Each child will produce a very personal puppet appropriate to his age or creative needs. While small children will prefer animals or characters from fairy tales, children of around ten will prefer to produce Indians, Vikings, pirates, comic-strip characters, or characters from books or television. This chapter is for parents who like to play and children who like to work. You will find that children regard concentrated and zealous activities as work when they are making puppets. You will notice their serious faces during work. Parents who work with their children should not influence their creativity; they should make their own puppets rather than meddle with their children's work. Obviously this does not mean that they should not lend a hand when difficulties arise, but this help should be restricted to technical problems. We are familiar with the following characters of the regular Punch-and-Judy shows, including their usual roles: Punch, Judy, grandmother, princess, and king. Your children will create entirely new possibilities for puppet shows when they are making their puppets.

Materials Needed

Most materials for making the puppets need not be bought; they are readily available in the home: two plastic buckets, old newspapers, wallpaper paste, cellophane tape, cardboard, plastic wood, high-grade binder, and poster colors or finger paints. (You can limit the colors to black, white, red, blue, and yellow, because all other colors can be mixed.) You will need flat-bristle brushes and somewhat finer camel's-hair brushes for painting the heads. For hair and beards you will need wool, hemp, crepe paper, feathers, and string, plus white glue for pasting. Clothes are sewn or glued from fabric remnants (size: twelve inches by thirty inches) and decorated with beads, braids, ribbons, buttons, etc.

Mixing

Approximately twenty minutes before you need it, mix wallpaper paste according to the instructions on the package. You will need about one quart of paste.

Let the paste stand for some time while the puppet's neck is being shaped. For this you need flexible cardboard. Cut a piece about two inches by four inches for each neck. Roll it around your finger, forming a tube two inches long, and glue it together with cellophane tape or white glue.

Then cover the working surface with newspapers; it is best to have rolled-up sleeves. Keep a stack of newspapers handy, and place a plastic bucket in the middle of the table. Each child

should take about four to eight pages of newspaper and tear it into long, thin strips, which are again shredded. Throw these shreds into the bucket. When the bucket is three-fourths full, pour part of the prepared paste in and stir the mixture with your hands or a wooden spoon.

The adult has to watch that the mixture does not get too wet and that the children, in their fervor, don't get paste all over their mouths and eyes.

Once the paste is ready, tear off a few thin strips of newspaper, as long as possible. These will be used later to wind around the heads to make them firm. Each worker should put aside a supply of strips, and then take a whole page of newspaper and crumple it into a ball. Now dip your hands in the prepared paste and rub them over the ball. Then place this ball on top of one of the cardboard necks and secure it by winding some of the prepared strips (if necessary, add more glue) around the head and neck.

Now shape the heads: make hollows for the eyes, shape the mouth, build the nose.

The puppet will become real
sculpture only after the final
coat of paste is applied. In this
way all the prominent parts are
formed, such as ears, nose,
chin, horns, cheeks, goggle
eyes, mouth. Wind additional
dry paper strips around any parts
that may not have become sufficiently solid because too much
glue was used. Once the final
shape has been established,

the head may be left to dry.
Mix the plastic wood with water
to a thick paste in a hard rubber
or plastic container. To make the
heads even more durable, add to
this paste some binder. Now
brush over the heads with a
flat-bristle brush, smoothing
their shapes and closing up
holes and cracks.

After the heads are completely dry, painting may be started. Adults should not interfere with the sometimes rather peculiar choice of colors by children; they should only explain beforehand the possibilities of color mixing and be sure the children wash their brushes each time before dipping in the color pots.

In order to find the necessary materials for clothing and decorating the puppets, it is worthwhile to search through sewing boxes, knitting baskets, toy chests, and drawers with odds and ends. No doubt one can find a lot that can be used.

Start with the decoration of the heads. Attach hair, eyebrows, beards, hats, and kerchiefs, according to taste and imagination.

Cut out the clothes from remnants of fabrics, approximately
twelve inches by thirty inches,
according to the striped sam-
ple shown in the photograph.
For a temporary solution, the
clothes can also be glued, but
it is better to sew them on a
machine or give the children
large, blunt needles and thread
so that they can sew the dresses
themselves with large stitches.

Leave a large hole at the neck.
Thread a long, woolen piece of
yarn in the opening, so it can
be pulled later to the desired
width.

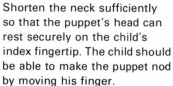

Shorten the neck sufficiently so that the puppet's head can rest securely on the child's index fingertip. The child should be able to make the puppet nod by moving his finger.

Now fit the puppet's neck in the neck opening of the dress, draw the string, and glue the material tightly to the cardboard. Tie the two ends of the yarn into a bow.

The Puppet Show

By playing, the child comes to terms with his surroundings and discovers his own methods of expressing and solving problems. Above all, puppet shows and playacting enable the child to present matters by which he is influenced every day, thus liberating him in a way. In order to represent his surroundings and problems by means of puppet shows, the child needs puppet actors. Puppets that are bought or puppets made by grown-ups are not as rewarding to a child as self-made ones. Only during the working process can the child visualize the appearance of the puppet and its characteristics if he is to act as its operator.

Parents who are capable of letting the child create as independently as possible, leaving the child in control, will be surprised at some of the products of their offspring. First of all, they will discover that the clown, the lion, the mouse, the princess, or the Indian usually somehow resembles its creator. Second, they will get better acquainted with their child by observing him as he works.

Working in Small Groups

The construction of a puppet is divided into many stages: forming, painting, sewing, and decorating. The entire process takes relatively long, at least two days. It would be best for parents of an only child to invite a few friends of their child to work together. The children will tackle the various tasks in different ways, and this could be the adult's chance to start group work. A beneficial exchange of talents will take place and the children should help each other. If the adult can achieve this, there will also be no argument when distributing clothes and trimmings. In short: the adult should enable the children to produce several beautiful puppets together. Personal achievements should be of no importance, and any competitive spirit among the children should be discussed; it should be emphasized that a well-made puppet is for everyone's benefit and the object is not to have made "the most beautiful one." The proper attitude should be that we are producing "our puppets," not each child "his puppet." This is excellent preparation for the combined efforts of the puppet show later on.

As a rule, only girls are familiar with the use of needle and thread, fabrics, yarn, beads, etc. The making of puppets offers a chance to persuade boys to do handcrafts. It would be a mistake for the adult to consider the making of clothes a task for girls only, since working with fabrics is particularly helpful in developing dexterity and a sense of touch, and this is just as important for boys as it is for girls.

For decorating the puppets you
might use beads, buttons, lace,
braid; these are all widely
available items. Many adorn-
ments may be made easily by

the child. For instance, crowns, chains, and other jewelry can be made out of silver foil. Or you may cut one-half to one-inch strips from the end of a roll of crepe paper. Slots can be cut into the strips at half-inch intervals; then the roll is opened up and you have wonderful fringes for bottom hems of skirts or for hair.

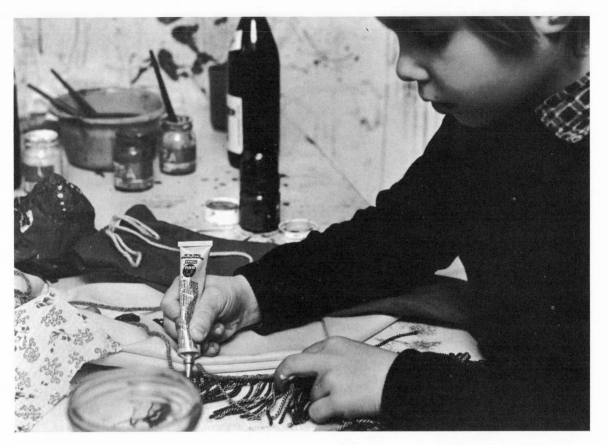

The children can twist their own cords from different colored yarn remnants. This is a special favorite with children. Cut the yarn in even lengths and place them on top of each other. Each end is held by one child, and they turn the strands in opposite directions. Once the strands are tightly rolled, one child takes both ends in one hand. The yarn will twist by itself. Then smooth out the cord and tie a knot at each end.

Scalloped borders, medals, and dots can be cut from colored felt; snowflakes are made of small dots of cotton. Crepe-paper flowers are made by gathering a circular piece of crepe paper in the middle. Narrow, frayed strips of fabric can be sewn on or glued on. Tassels are made by winding yarn over two fingers, wrapping a strand around one end of this bundle, and then cutting the other end. Frayed strands of string can be used for wisps of hair, eyebrows, and curls.

In case the children want to make extra-beautiful decorations, here are sketches of a few simple embroidery stitches that may be used. It is best to let the children work with cotton yarn and large darning needles without sharp points. This yarn is best because it does not fray, and therefore it is easier for a child to thread.

Take care that the children keep the fabric as taut as possible when they are embroidering.

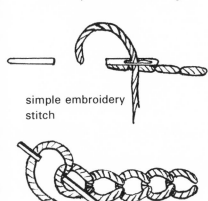

simple embroidery stitch

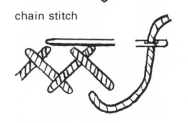

chain stitch

herringbone stitch

You will notice that the moment the paper balls are attached to the tops of the cardboard necks, the children start to play with the puppets. During the process of working on the puppets the children will take time out to play with them, and one should not interrupt them. Later on, the children should play with the puppets just as spontaneously as they did during the working process.

4. WEAVING WITH PAPER AND WOOL

by Irmgard Muenk and Illo von Rauch-Wittlich

The instructions contained in this chapter will serve primarily as stimulation, they do not embrace the entire field of braiding and weaving. The examples have been adjusted according to the age and aptitude of children; they should appeal to and provide enjoyment for younger as well as older children. At first weaving may appear to be just hard work, leaving little scope for ideas or games. We want to show that an abundance of enjoyable ideas may be expressed with this particular technique. Braiding and weaving are best done with small groups. Parents with only one child should invite one or more children to participate, if possible.

Materials Needed

A variety of papers may be used for the beginning: drawing paper, colored paper, crepe paper, cellophane, silver foil, tinfoil, colored cardboard, paper streamers, illustrated magazines, plastics, oilcloth, toilet paper, and newspapers. Some of these materials may be found in the home; there is no need to buy expensive materials. You will also need a pair of scissors, glue, cellophane tape, a ruler, and possibly a stapler. The best possible working surface is a large table or the floor. After completion, delicate materials have to be protected with transparent plastic sheets.

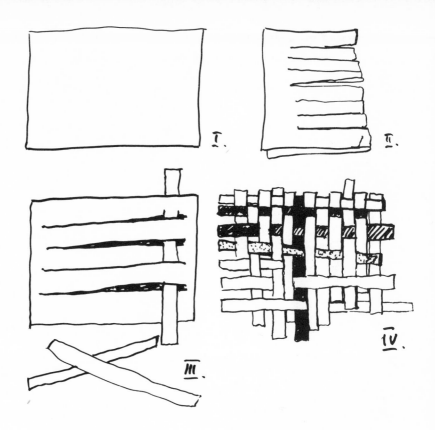

Weaving with Paper

In order to become familiar with the technique, we will start with paper, since the technique for using this material is easiest to explain.

Interweaving

Fold a sheet of paper in the middle, so that the two halves lie on top of each other. Make incisions with the scissors starting from the fold up to shortly before the outside edges (*drawing I*). The distance between the cuts should be one-eighth to three-fourths inch. Then take another sheet of equal size, fold it in the middle, and repeat the process, except this time cut the strips all the way through.

63

Now spread out the first paper grid and open it flat on the working surface. Then weave one of the prepared strips through the grid, beneath the first strip, over the second strip, beneath the third one, etc. Both ends of the braiding strip should be left protruding (*drawing III*). Once the first strip has been woven through, it should be pushed against the outer edge. Now work may start with the second strip. It should be explained to the child that where the first strip is placed underneath the paper, the next one should be above: in short, that there should be a constant alternation. Once the job of weaving is completed, the ends of the strips should be pasted to the margin of the paper grid; the rest is cut off.

Suggestions for Uses

Cut out a square piece of cardboard a little smaller than the completed woven paper. Glue this wickerwork creation to the cardboard, leaving an even margin on all sides. Cut off the four protruding corners; turn over the margins and glue them to the back of the cardboard. Carefully cover the entire surface with transparent, self-adhesive plastic. The result is a gay place mat. Weaving done with colored plastics can be made into an attractive window decoration.

Once the children have learned the basic techniques, they may be encouraged to do their own designing. They might like to learn how to make pigtails, for example. They should be shown that the same basic principle again applies: alternate up-and-down strips. Long rolls of toilet paper or crepe paper may be used for practice. Many games may be devised by dressing up with long, colorful braids.

It is also rewarding to encourage the children to create improvised combinations of painting and weaving. Irregular weaving into a paper base can produce surprising effects. Other suitable materials are heavy string, drinking straws, and bias tape. The children in this group, for instance, have invented a "hedgehog," which was later changed into a sun. Drinking straws were inserted into a styrofoam ball, producing the hedgehog. Later on they covered it with a wickerwork of bast and bias tape and it became a brightly colored sun.

A Simple Weaving Frame

In order to produce the simplest kind of weaving frame, each child should take an oblong piece of strong cardboard and make one-fourth-inch incisions with the scissors at regular intervals of one-fourth inch to one-half inch on two opposite sides. Now the children take a ball of heavy string, attach it with a knot under the first incision, and start stretching it across the cardboard (*see drawing*). All frames suggested here are covered the same way. Once the frame is completely covered with continuous lengths of string, the string is fastened with a knot and cut off. This completes the warp.

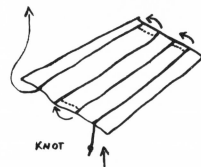

KNOT

Weaving

This frame may be used for a variety of materials. To avoid monotony, the children may be encouraged to use a variety of materials and weaving strips in many colors. The principle is the same as when weaving with paper. Again, the children have to take great care that the beginning of any new row is correct, so that the strips alternate. The material to be used for weaving is made into a firm ball, so that it can be pulled through easily.

A further aid is a thin ruler or narrow piece of cardboard, which will facilitate the lifting of the warp, just as on a real loom.

Materials for Weaving

Frame weaving may be done with any flexible material, such as wool, ribbons, yarn, strips of fabric, thread, as well as heavy string, straw, wood shavings (available in hobby shops), drinking straws, etc. From yarn additional weaving materials can be made: thick strands may be twisted and used for further weaving. Cut equal lengths of yarn and place them on top of each other. Each end is held by one child and the strands are twisted in opposite directions until they are tightly rolled. Then one child takes both ends in one hand and the threads will twist on their own. Smooth out and knot the strands together at the ends.

Here are two more weaving frames made in the same way as the first one. One is a wooden frame that was purchased and the other is a homemade cardboard frame. Both have incisions along two sides. Children can easily copy the homemade frame.

Further materials suitable for weaving may be found on a nature walk. You may find rushes, long blades of grass, stems, leaves, feathers, and much more to enhance a piece of weaving. Occasionally even fine metal or silver wire may be used to make woven pieces of jewelry.

Braiding and Weaving

The working method is basically the same for all the materials mentioned. Each material may be used with the techniques described. All materials have one thing in common: flexibility. Usually the adult instructor has preconceived, limited ideas of braiding and weaving. The more deviation from the ordinary examples, the better the results. Soon the children will prove that braiding and weaving can be a lot of fun rather than reminiscent of medieval weaving rooms or boring handcraft lessons.

Today's educators aim to stimulate both girls and boys in equal activities. This also tends to equalize the different abilities due to education. Needlework is not an inborn, specifically female talent, and perhaps this book will help to eliminate this prejudice. The objects produced here were the result of a common venture and enjoyment for boys and girls together.

Working in Small Groups

In the beginning success is mostly the responsibility of the adult. He has to create interest for the planned undertaking without demanding excessive achievements and performance. Even in a group you have to pay attention to each child, i.e., practice with him the basic techniques until he understands and is capable of continuing on his own. This way you may prevent problems that would otherwise demoralize the child.

The main problem for the adult is to estimate the proper amount of attention to be allotted to each child and at the same time to provide step-by-step guidance for the whole group. Once they all understand the principle of weaving, they should be encouraged to invent their own creations. Here the adult should not try to influence the children, because the joy of making unusual combinations of materials, which normally would not go together, is far more important than conventional ideas. The adult should limit his influence to starting group work, and he should avoid giving special praise to individual children. Instead, he should demonstrate how the entire group can execute tasks that could never be achieved by a single child.

Wooden Weaving Frames

The wooden frame shown here is another one that can be made by children who are already capable of using a hammer and nails. Saw a long strip of wooden molding into four equal parts, and nail the sections together at the corners. Then drive in nails at the same distances as on the other frames, with the longer part of the nail protruding but nevertheless firmly fixed.

Now cover the frame with the warp wound around the nails, just as with the other frames. The frame shown here was woven with drinking straws and pieces of straw.

It is also possible to weave smaller pieces on this large frame either by not covering all the nails, or by detaching the piece when it has reached the desired size. (The technique for removing the work from the frame is described later.) It should be obvious to the instructor when the children's patience is exhausted, and he should not demand too much.

With smaller children, therefore, it would be better to weave string rugs for a doll house, or small purses, objects for which the child can foresee the conclusions. There is nothing more disappointing for all participants than abandonment of a half-finished project.

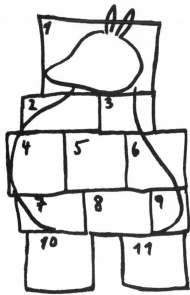

Cooperative Weaving

You may also want to encourage a whole group to weave something together. It should be something that all the children can use together. The children shown working in this chapter got the idea of making a wall hanging with sewn-on pockets for storing their toys and painting materials.

In order to obtain a funny shape, they decided to weave a kangaroo. Adults who are weaving with children for the first time should start with small group projects made up of simple rectangular parts. The kangaroo we made was first sketched on cardboard,

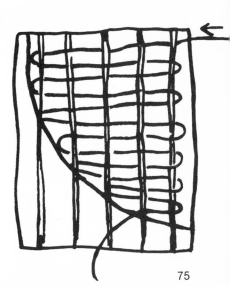

In order to facilitate the weaving of the outside curves, this figure was divided into many clearly arranged rectangles, some partly protruding beyond the outlines of the figure. The rectangles are then cut out, and for each of them a small weaving frame is built, as explained in the beginning. Now weaving can proceed according to the drawing. The finished piece is always somewhat smaller than the weaving frame, because it is necessary to use about two inches of the warp to lift the piece off the frame.

Lifting the Woven Piece off the Frame

Take the woven piece off the frame by pulling off and cutting the loops on the side worked last. Knot them, leaving a fringed margin.

Now the children assemble the separate pieces for the kangaroo. Here they sew them together with large, blunt, needles and appliqué the eyes, ears, and mouth. In the end the work is attached to a piece of cardboard cut to size. Now the kangaroo is finished and the children proudly claim ownership.

5. PAINTED STONES AND STONE SCULPTURES

by Nina Agerholm

A child's first encounter with the raw material of unshaped stones comes when he is crawling on the floor or playing in the sandbox. Stones are cold, hard, heavy, rough or smooth, round or angular. The child gets to know something about paints around the beginning of the third year; he is acquainted first with finger paints, later on with colored pencils, and then with paints that are applied with a brush.

At first the child paints flat surfaces that are limited on top, bottom, and sides: pictures. With the painting of stones a new dimension is added: stones have many sides and surfaces and no two of them are alike. The shape of a stone varies according to the viewing angle.

● Experience: center of gravity and balance.
A stone does not always remain in the position desired. If it is put down on its larger surface, it will remain in position, but if it is placed on its smallest side, it will easily topple over when pushed.

● Experience: perspective. Stones are nothing special when a lot of them are lying around outside. If they are brought into the house and decorated, they may well become minor works of art.

● Experience: the possibility of shaping one's environment. For some children this is not a new experience, but it is brought to the foreground by playful handling of the material. Colors are the first optical stimulus for a small child. Form is added much later, finally forming an optical unit: the red ball; the green car, the blue building block. In this order the child's creativity will develop.

At first the child will paint curves, circles, ovals, wavy lines, straight lines, and shapes without any purpose or concept. The child merely enjoys the motions of following a certain inner-directed stimulus, thus making it possible to create a colored surface from a plain one.

The child's experience of motion by transferring color to paper with his own two hands is more and more pushed aside by the ever-new creative results. The next logical step is the painting of objects, i.e., adding another dimension. This will give more latitude to the child's kinetic drive, previously limited by painting only flat surfaces. Stones may be rotated and turned. However, this natural chain is often interrupted by the grown-up, whether out of ignorance ("What is this supposed to be?") or misplaced ambition ("Try to paint the man in the moon."). The child is forced to produce a seemingly measurable result, even before he can develop his own creative powers.

The unrestricted painting of stones varying in shapes and sizes with different textures, detached from any forced creativity, provides the child with knowledge that could otherwise only be gained by laborious theory if this important phase of development were skipped. He would be deprived of the chance to grasp something by his own observation in the true sense of the word. To demonstrate this, here is just one example: two identical cobblestones are painted in two different solid colors—one yellow and the other brown. Result: the yellow stone will appear to be lighter in weight than the brown one and the light-colored stone will appear to be larger than the dark one.

● Experience: influence through choice of color (color effect).

By close association with stones and colors the child is continuously inspired to new creative impulses, so that eventually he uses decorative elements on his own, such as patterns (dots, stripes, crosses, waves, and zigzag lines), ornaments, and figurative representations. Of course the shape of the stone will also have to be considered—especially if it happens to be particularly suited to the purpose of design. However, independent considerations stemming from a characteristic stone formation cannot be expected of preschool children. A grown-up has to encourage such ideas. But once a child has been shown the right way, he will have no problems in subjugating his painting to the shape of the stone and working out its form more clearly by painting. Since the child's imagination differs considerably from the grown-up's, it is important that one does not force one's own ideas on the child. If, for instance, the child wants to discover the shape of a boot in a stone, then it is a boot, even if you rather envision it as a sitting cat. Seeing and recognizing certain shapes will train the feeling for details and subconsciously teach discriminating methods of observation. Any kind of game presents an important learning process for the child. Thus, the experiences when working with stones and colors are actually only marginal. The emphasis is on the enjoyment of the unrestricted occupation with materials suitable for children. This will provide the experience of success, which is so important in the development of a personality.

Working Conditions

Children require a lot of working space. They should be able to spread out. The best possible place is the floor, which should be covered with newspapers (not plastic bags, they are slippery). It is best to choose a room, or at least a corner of a room, where the child may interrupt work without having to clear away everything. A large bathroom, easy to clean up, is ideal for using paints, water, stones, sand, and glue. In summer, of course, work may also proceed outdoors. It is important to give the child sufficient time to work, so no project should be started an hour before a meal or shortly before bedtime.

Materials Needed

First of all, you will need stones, many of them, so that the child has ample choice and a chance to practice on several pieces at the same time. It would be a mistake to make the child work uninterruptedly. Difficulties in solving a problem will limit and stifle the imagination. A small child's feeling for details is not yet developed, and larger surfaces are therefore preferable.
In addition to the stones, which should be collected with the children, you will need paints.

For children between two and four, fingerpaints are best. They are particularly smooth and may be rubbed or smeared on by hand. These paints are not poisonous. Older children may prefer to use either colored wax crayons or water-soluble paints, like poster colors or tempera. The brushes should be ordinary flat bristle brushes in various widths. Further necessities are wooden sticks for stirring the paint, plastic containers for mixing, perhaps some paste to make water colors smearproof (or india ink), and colorless varnish. For stone mosaics and stone sculptures you will need white glue and sand for bonding, tinfoil or plastic wrap, and a container with straight sides (a box or the lid of a can) to use as a mold.

Proper clothing should be worn while painting. Smocks made of heavy plastic shopping bags are ideal, and they are free. In addition they are fun to wear. Simply cut semicircles in the two lower corners to form the armholes, and a large opening in the middle of the bottom for the head.

First the stones have to be thoroughly scrubbed with a hard brush in plenty of water. Then put them in fresh water, add detergent, and wash them once more to remove any trace of oil or grease. Paint will not adhere properly on a greasy surface. Dry the stones well and let them dry thoroughly for quite a while longer. Then the children should choose the stones they want to work with.

At first these will be mostly round shapes with smooth surfaces, because they are the best transition from the familiar flat painted surfaces of paper, cardboard, or blackboard.

There are no problems with finger paints, which should be used for younger children or children without former painting experience. The paint is simply scooped out of the containers by hand and spread over

the stones. This method does not yet represent decorative painting of a surface. The primary aim of most children is to paint a stone completely, to cover it entirely, thereby gaining their first experience with a new medium. If the child wants to paint the stone on another side, he has to wait

for the painted surface to dry first, otherwise the paint will come off. If one does not watch the child carefully, the stone will not be covered entirely with paint. If several colors are painted on top of each other, new hues will result.

For the younger children the results of their efforts are of no great importance. Though they will paint the stone with abandon, their pleasure is brief, and they will very soon turn their attention to another stone. They also don't mind washing off the paint that has just been applied with great care and starting all over again. As mentioned in the beginning, there is more enjoyment in unlimited activity than in achieving a final result. Should the outcome of such painting seem quite attractive to an adult, this is usually only accidental. This could also be regarded as "passive creativity." Active creativity, purposeful design, is a gradual process. It is supported and promoted by the dexterity and understanding gained during haphazard work.

Painting with a Brush

Liquid paints are applied with a brush. The most suitable colors are the so-called casein-emulsion paints. Paints kept in small glasses may be thinned down and mixed. They do not smear after drying, and they may be covered with colorless varnish to increase their luminosity. However, this should not be done by children of preschool age without adult supervision. Paints from school paint boxes are less suitable for painting on stones because they are not opaque enough. Tempera paints mixed with water can be made smear-proof by adding special glue. When using watercolors, keep a large, firmly fixed container of water nearby to clean the brushes every so often.

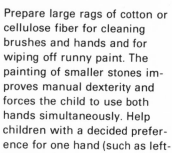

Prepare large rags of cotton or cellulose fiber for cleaning brushes and hands and for wiping off runny paint. The painting of smaller stones improves manual dexterity and forces the child to use both hands simultaneously. Help children with a decided preference for one hand (such as left-handed ones) to train the neglected hand. Color does not always have to be brushed on; it may also be sprayed on by holding a brush well saturated with paint close to the surface to be painted and blowing at it. Thin paint may also be dripped from various heights, creating large and small dots. Such dots may also be made by stippling with an almost-dry brush. If drawings with thin outlines are desired, they can be done very well with wax crayons or chalks, but only if the surface to be painted has a light background and is smooth. Otherwise the painting will be hardly recognizable.

Dark stones may be covered first with light watercolor. This primer also serves to close some of the pores and provides a more solid ground. As a rule there are not too many stones that obviously resemble an object or creature recognized by a child. Here, some encouragement to think is advisable. You don't have to wait until you find a stone that has an obvious shape that may be recognized; it is sufficient to tell the child that a round stone looks like a mouse, and the child will react immediately. If it is a small child, he will look for more mouse-stones. If he is older, he will develop his own imagination and perhaps make some corrections, such as, "This one looks rather like a hedgehog." This opens up the way to conscious looking and recognizing. A less talented child may be inspired by several suggestions as to the shape of a stone, but the final decision should be left to the child.

The next step, after seeing and recognizing, is the transposition of the mental image into a visible one through color. In contrast to free design, here the shape of the stone is considered while painting. This does not mean that the outlines should be followed, but the painting should supplement its characteristic shape. Every child will first paint a face on an oval stone. This concept of the round shape of a head is due less to looking at the people surrounding the child than to observation of his dolls or toy animals—again by imitation.

Only gradually will a child recognize a somewhat familiar head shape in an angular stone. When looking at a large triangular stone, the adult might think of a tent or house with a pointed roof. Not so a child. The object demonstrated here and carefully painted is a slice of a giant coconut pie.

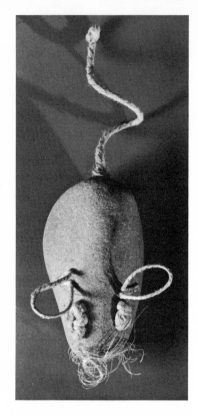

Stone Sculptures

Small sculptures can be made with stones of various sizes. The stones for such sculptures are glued to each other with a paste made of white glue and sand (two parts glue and one part sand). Care has to be taken to glue only larger surfaces to each other to keep them firm. The production of stone sculptures puts equal demands on the imagination and skill, as there are so many possible combinations. Form, size, colors, or surface structures of stones permit infinite variety, which may even be supplemented with paint or additional materials, as shown on the mouse.

The stones have to be thoroughly dry before use. For a child's first attempt it is best to offer occasional advice, so that the child will not become discouraged right away by possible failures. A child is not capable of anticipating technical difficulties. It is best to start with two rocks to be glued to each other. If they are small and therefore light stones, they can be pressed together after gluing until the glue is dry. Larger stones, where more glue has to be used, are best left to dry in a corner, supported by other objects. If a sculpture is to be made out of three stones, the two bottom ones are glued together first. After they are dry, the next stone is added. With sculptures made of four stones, the two lower ones are glued first, then the two upper ones. After both of the joins are dry, the two stone pairs are glued to each other. During this process the child will learn to work systematically and start to think in terms of three dimensions. He will also train his feeling for harmony and proportion.

Though the child should be left to his own devices, as in all creative activities, he should be made aware of the independent effects of color and structure of stones, while painting, so that he can learn the distinctions between natural and decorative effects.

Stone Mosaics

Mosaics are made of small stones imbedded in cement. These stones may be used in their natural colors or they may be painted beforehand. Any container with straight sides may be used as a mold for the cement. It will only be used as a mold and will therefore not become damaged. First line the inside of this mold with tinfoil or silver paper, all the way up on the sides. Mix a cement of white glue and fine-grain sand (birdcage sand or beach sand) in a plastic container, forming a thick paste. Cover the bottom of the mold with this paste, making it a little deeper than a child's thumb. If the bottom area is larger than a dinner plate, make the layer of cement thicker.

Press the well-cleaned stones into the mixture; then sprinkle sand over the entire surface and let it harden. Depending on the thickness of the layer, this will take a few hours or a whole night. Afterward the mosaic may be carefully tipped out of the mold.

6. SELF-STICKING PLASTICS

by Karin Walther

Self-sticking plastics are suitable for children of three and up. Even clumsy children can do no harm, since crooked and badly cut pieces will still be effective due to their luminosity. Furthermore, anything may be changed, since the sheets may be unstuck easily. Once the various processes have been demonstrated, the children should be left to their own devices. They may have entirely different ideas about how to use the plastic sheets. Share their enjoyment in any of the results obtained, and do not spoil there pleasure by asking them to produce a certain pattern according to your own imagination.

Materials Needed

Self-adhesive plastics in transparent colors are something special, because they can produce a magical world of magnificent opalescence. The colors can be blended by sticking pieces on top of each other or next to each other. They never appear gray, and they produce any desired hue. There are also contact papers, colored self-adhesive plastics with a shiny or a matte surface. They are odorless and nontoxic; they are resilient and do not tear easily; they may be rolled; and they are resistant to cold and heat. The easiest working method is obviously to stick the pieces on top of each other, since they may be peeled off and reused as often as desired. They are washable and resistant to harmless acids or oils. Plastics are insoluble when applied over paper. They adhere strongly to glass, plexiglass, oilcloth, or any other synthetic products, and they may be removed without leaving a trace. Another advantage of this craft is that few tools are required. Many projects can be executed by children with a special rounded-end pair of scissors, nail scissors, and a hole punch. If perfectly round circles are desired, round objects—such as large

coins, cups, or soup bowls—may be used. Other items that may stimulate the children's imagination are plastic or metal snap fasteners, self-sticking labels, and reinforcement rings.

You can buy self-sticking plastic and transparent sheets in many colors, also contact paper in various thicknesses, in any art supply store or hobby shop. Self-sticking labels, reinforcement rings, ball-point pens, and felt pens are available in any stationery store or department store. Children's scissors with rounded ends are available in any toy department. You will find plastic sheets and oilcloth and other synthetic materials in department or hardware stores. Hardware stores or department stores also carry plastic shopping bags, containers for mixing, inexpensive glasses, containers made of plastic or cardboard, plates, cups, plus plastic cushions, life preservers, plastic umbrellas, all of which may be covered imaginatively. In your own home you may find plastic containers, yogurt containers, empty coffee or jam jars, which may well be decorated.

Cutting Out Plastics

Most children are able to cut narrow and wide strips from a sheet with a free hand. This task does not require preliminary sketching. Small rectangles and squares are the first shapes, the first elements, and at the same time the first ornaments. Less complicated forms are easier to cut out. Detach the protective backing, arrange the pieces, and stick them in place. Here the child is making a diagonal cut in the rectangle or square, thus obtaining a triangle.

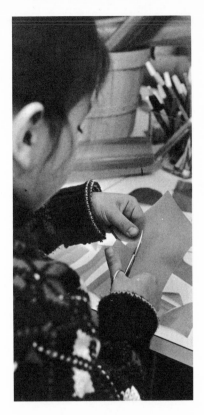

More advanced children may start to practice round cuts with curved nail scissors. The first incision will be sickle shaped. It takes practice to cut completely round forms. If an accurate circle is desired, coffee cups, yogurt containers, or other round objects may be used.

These patterns should be firmly placed on the reverse side of the sheets; the outlines should be drawn by the child with a ball-point or felt pen.

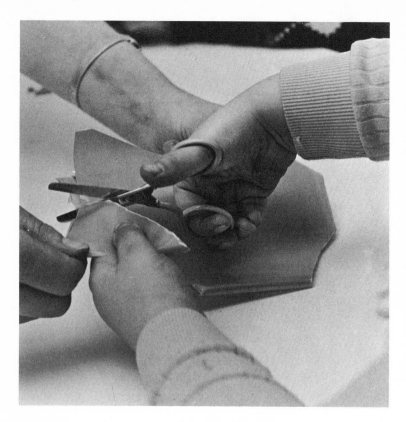

Folded Cuts

Children enjoy cutting into two or three layers of plastic sheets. In the beginning several layers are somewhat hard to cut. Children of three and four perhaps should not cut more than two layers at a time. When the folded forms are opened up, children are surprised to see the very even and symmetrical ornaments that result.

Confetti

There are unlimited possibilities in making ornaments with confetti. At the end of this chapter are photographs of a few of the many possibilities of producing a picture out of these round bits of paper; and they show how separate elements may be combined with perforated sheets. The use of the hole punch requires some training. Let the children practice on their own for a while. Very small children will usually use both hands to tackle the lever in a single movement. If it is done too slowly, the sheets will become crumpled and sticky and hard to move. If the bottom of the punch is removed, the homemade confetti will drop on the table.

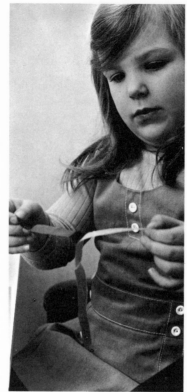

absorbed, even by pulling off the backing of the tiny confetti. Larger pieces are best handled by two children. One child holds on to the sheet with both hands—see the illustration here—while the other one makes a small slit at the corner and then, very carefully and slowly, pulls off the entire backing so that the material does not stick to itself and creases are avoided. With more complicated forms, such as folded cuts, the children should be helped. If no help is given and the cutout decorations stick to each other, the child may soon become discouraged, lose patience, and no longer enjoy the work.

Removing the Protective Backing

Once the basic forms are cut out, they may be affixed to a flat surface. For this purpose, the protective backing on the plastic sheets has to be pulled off. However, this should not be done before the single parts are arranged on the foundation to be used for the picture.

Then the protective backing should be pulled off and the child can start to stick down the material. The children should be shown how to separate the backing from the plastic sheets by making a tiny slit in the edge. They don't always succeed right away with their small, often clumsy hands, but once children understand how it is done, they soon become completely

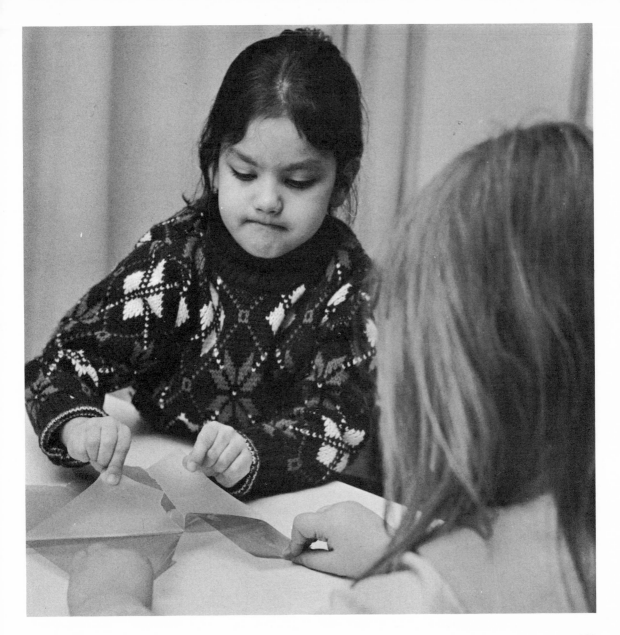

various colors against a window and placing them on top of each other. They can practice blending the primary colors first. The quickest method of demonstrating how the colors will intersect and blend by being applied on top of each other or next to each other is to let the children stick colored pieces on a pane of glass. Here, unlike regular opaque colors, secondary colors will never lose their luminosity through blending. The effect is always cheerful, whether one is looking through the window from the inside or the outside. The many ornaments are produced by various techniques. They were spontaneously positioned by looking toward the light, and this resulted in an "enchanted" playroom window. Since transparent plastics are fascinating to handle, children create their own magnificent color effects by sticking the pieces over or next to each other. They may start by using simple elements, such as strips, rectangles, triangles, or circles, and you will be surprised how quickly children will compose pictures by arranging, shifting, and overlapping the shapes.

Attaching and Combining

The process of sticking down the papers is a lot of fun for children, since it is then that the effect of the decorative and spatial combination shows up and becomes "transparent." This also serves as an inspiration for playing with colors. A three-dimensional effect may be achieved, for instance, by sticking several pictorial elements on top of each other. This will add to the depth of the picture. Take care that not too many colors are used in the beginning. The primary colors are yellow, red, and blue. Orange, violet, and green (secondary colors) may be obtained by blending two at a time. This may be demonstrated to the children by holding sheets of

Self-Adhesive Reinforcement Rings and Labels

In order to increase their choice of possibilities and materials, children may produce mosaics of self-adhesive labels and reinforcement rings. These ready-made decorations are particularly useful as features of people or birds. The rings may become eyes for a doll or buttons for a dress. Other self-adhesive labels may also be used. However, care should be taken to offer the children only the basic elements, allowing them to add their own designs. They should not rush to complete pictures that will be forgotten after a few minutes, their only attraction having been the task of attaching them.

Working with Snap Fasteners

The parts of the large doll shown here are connected with snap fasteners. A similar method may be used for a crocodile, a ship, a fish, a small satchel, a dragon, or a very long train.

Holes are punched in each part and then fastened to each other with snap fasteners. One half of the fastener is pushed underneath the prepunched cutting edge and inserted, then the other part—also prepunched— is pressed on from top. This method works well for all designs made with several components. The children enjoy this because the components may be moved and are interchangeable. This becomes a special game.

 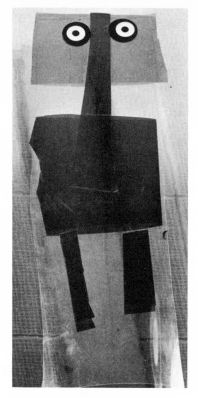

working in a group. If you give one color to each child, they can interchange them and, no doubt, all the extra pieces will be utilized. By exchanging sheets of plastic, by sharing the hole punch, by using the scissors together, children will learn early in life how to get along with each other and gain the experience of community work while playing, as in any kind of group occupation. However, it is up to the adult to distribute his assistance equally among the children. Fragile children may require a little more attention and aid, but they are often capable of producing quietly small works of art. In that case praise and encouragement may be reassuring and liberating.

Basic shapes may become small works of art. Here a circle and several rectangles have been cut out, and already there is Alexander himself, the boy who made the picture. Next to it is a giraffe, looking particularly funny because of the two reinforcement rings attached alongside the extended nose. Several of these cheerful primitive figures have been com-

bined by children in a group to form a mobile, as shown here. Holes were punched into the colored pieces of plexiglass, and they were hung up by threads attached to a stick or piece of bamboo. If hung in front of a window, the slightest breeze will create ever-new opalescence.

Self-adhesive plastics are particularly suitable for children

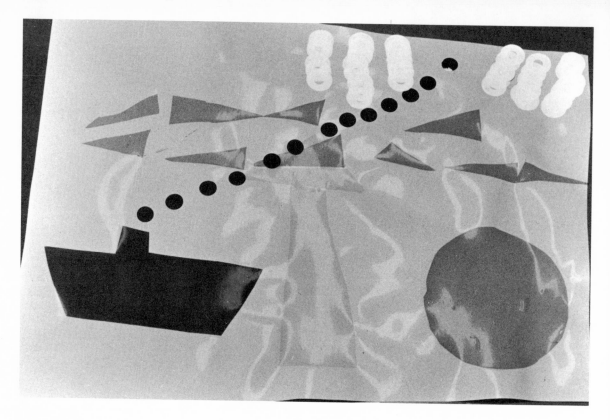

You can actually "paint" with transparent plastics and create an abundance of pictures merely by combining small pieces and decorative elements. In the beginning it may be advisable to suggest a few subjects in order to inspire the children. There is great variety in fairy tales, or maybe the children recently saw something interesting in the street. What do they remember from their last vacation? Suggestions such as these will be quite sufficient to inspire busy cutting out, shifting of cutout pieces, and diligent assembling. This wonderful ship, for instance, is surrounded by triangular waves and is "swimming" on a plastic sheet. The long black smoke of confetti is blowing toward the reinforcement rings, and surely the large red ball was thrown off the ship by a little girl.

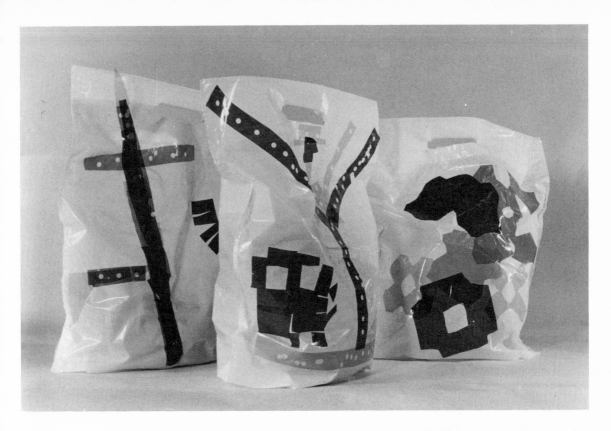

Self-adhesive plastics may also serve as ideal decorations for many useful objects. Welcome gifts for Mother's Day are plastic shopping bags decorated with simple shapes, especially since they make a nice change from the usual unimaginative plastic bags. Translucent covers and letter files can be decorated by even the smallest children.

114

A Children's Party

Children may attach table and room decorations to glasses, paper plates, bottles, and cups, thus creating their own individual setting. This might even be done as a game during the party, and in the end each child might take home as a souvenir "his glass" or whatever he produced. The flexible sheets may be removed easily from any smooth surface. Plastic containers are most suitable for simple jobs. They may be decorated with all kinds of scraps. If a small stick or a knitting needle is stuck in the middle and fastened, they even make wonderful heads for an improvised puppet theater. No doubt the children will have no problem in animating their containers and creating a clown, a cat, Punch and Judy, or other characters. Lastly, colorfully covered balloons may be distributed to serve as both decorations and toys.

7. BALLOONS AND PAPIER-MACHE

by Elisabeth Gloor

stimulation by the adult. The younger the child, the more he will prefer a demonstration to a verbal explanation. It is therefore best for an adult to sit down at the table and start working on a project. He can then explain the process at the same time, and he will always be present if the child needs help. However, he should not produce actual models himself, but merely make suggestions. It is very important for a child to be able to realize his own conceptions independently. Independence in choosing, handling, constructing, and designing stimulates the child's creativity; it trains his sense of observation and improves his manual skill. In the course of creating an object from raw material to finished product, his imagination will increase and develop. Thus the working process is more important than the final product. The values of exactness, sense of reality, or usefulness are immaterial to children between the ages of three and eight.

Applying paste to balloons has been done in several stages, since each layer of paste always has to dry. It is therefore possible to work over periods of from two to three days, according to the children's perseverance. This is a suitable technique for small groups. According to their ages, the children will either tear the paper, apply the paste or paint, or improve the designs.

Materials Needed

Balloons, a round container (a bowl, can, or jar), old newspapers, wallpaper paste, a bucket or small tub for mixing, a spoon for stirring.

By using paper, fabric, paste, etc., to decorate balloons, a child will become familiar with the materials and will try to change and combine them according to his imagination. Once the possibilities are exhausted, the child will need further

Preparation of Working Surface

Cover a table with newspapers. Prepare chairs for the children to sit or kneel on. Cover the floor with newspapers or cardboard. This kind of prepara- is always advisable, whether the children are working in the nursery, kitchen, or play-room. Working with wallpaper paste always holds all kinds of temptations to experiment, and it is a pity if the children have to be reminded constantly to be careful of the furniture. This might dampen their activi-ties unnecessarily, and it also might have a restraining effect on their eagerness to experi-ment, which is eactly what should be encouraged.

Mixing the Paste

Wallpaper paste is available in hobby shops, in hobby de-partments of department stores, in paint stores, or in drugstores. A five-ounce package is suffi-cient for decorating six to ten large balloons. Mix the powder with water, according to the package instructions, and let it stand for twenty minutes.

Tearing Up Newspaper

In the meantime, newspapers should be ripped up. Ordinary daily papers are most suitable, since they are absorbent and of lower quality than some Sunday papers. Small children often have difficulty tearing a whole sheet in small strips. It may be best to proceed in stages. First tear a double sheet of newspaper into two parts at the center fold, then tear each one in half, and then in half once again. Each child should tear up about six double pages of a newspaper into the size of a notebook and stack them in the middle of the table, together with the other children's sheets. After all the newspapers have been torn to the same size, each sheet is torn in small strips. A few sheets may be left in the notebook size for sausage-shaped balloons. The rounder the balloon, the narrower the strips (three-eighths to three-fourths inch), to prevent creases on the surface of the balloon.

Inflating the Balloons

How easily a balloon bursts during play! So each child should get at least three. They are obtainable in stationery shops, toy shops, and department stores.

To facilitate inflation of the balloons for smaller children, an adult should blow up the balloon first and then release the air, except for a small amount. Once the balloon has reached the desired size, or the largest possible size, it is sealed with a simple knot. Let the children play freely with the inflated balloons. This is the way to experience it as an object and become acquainted with its characteristics (light, thin-walled, floating), which will be completely changed later on by the added decorations.

Applying Paste to the Balloons

After twenty minutes' wait,
the paste should be stirred vigor-
ously. It should then be placed
in the center of the table within
easy reach of all children, or
poured into individual small
containers, as shallow as possible, in which the children
can immerse their hands. Wallpaper paste is nonpoisonous;

it may be removed from hands
and clothes with water.
In order to leave both hands free
for applying the paste, the
balloon should be placed on
a round bowl. Then one paper
strip after another should be
covered with paste, until the
paper is well saturated, stuck
to the balloon, and smoothed
out with both hands. Avoid protruding ends and creases. If

newsprint is available, alter-
nating layers of printed and
unprinted paper may be applied.
Then the children are able to
count the number of layers
they have applied. This way,
the thickness of the paper skin
will also be more even.

After two or three layers of paper have been applied, the entire form is again covered with paste and left to dry on a sheet of newspaper, or hung up by the uncovered end of the balloon. It will take two days to dry in normal room temperature, but considerably less time in the sun. Be careful when leaving it close to a strong heat source; this will heat up the air inside the balloon, and it will expand and burst.

The pasting should be done in three stages, totaling six to eight layers of paper. When fingers no longer leave an impression on the dry skin, it is thick enough. The end of the balloon is pushed inside the paper skin or pulled out with the balloon. The opening is pasted over with a few strips.

The Balloon Becomes a Shape

According to the child's development and interests, the basic form will remain, in his eyes, a balloon or a ball. No pressure should be used. Without any substantial transformation, it might become a rattle, an egg, a Chinese lantern, or a puppet.

This basic form, however, may spontaneously inspire older children to create shapes differing from the original balloon. It is always interesting to observe how much the thought, vision, and experience of an adult differs from a child's. You may be reminded of a pear, while the child envisions a beetle, or a baby carriage, or a goblin. Some children need incentives to create something of their own out of the basic shape. They require incentives to see and think, but not to work. Adults should avoid meddling with the often self-willed and original imagination of a child. All too often a child will accept a concept forced upon him by an adult, thus paralyzing his own creative activities. An adult should encourage the child to act independently, and intervene only when aid is needed for solving technical problems. Problems that are beyond the child's knowledge and dexterity

are discouraging, and this is the time when adult assistance is needed.

Spontaneous work eliminates the need for preliminary sketching on paper. Children between three and six years do not see a connection between the two-dimensional figure on paper and the three-dimensional one that they are holding in their hands. Their mental image of what they want to create is constantly changing, expanding, and crystallizing while they work with a medium. Some inspiration should be given to indecisive children, but afterward they should have an opportunity to deal with their work, to become absorbed, in order to create something all their own.

Additional Parts to be Pasted to the Basic Shape

These may consist of various scrap materials available in any household. According to the figure the child wants to create, he can use:
—cardboard tubes,
—cans,
—cardboard boxes,
—egg cartons, etc.

Additional parts can also be made by the child from paper and paste. According to the size required, a small sheet or several pages of newspaper can be crumpled into a loose ball, which is wrapped up with another piece of newspaper, well covered with paste. With some dexterity, the whole ball can be molded into any desired shape. If various shapes are required, newspaper should be cut up and mashed with paste to a fairly dry pulp. Out of this, more delicate shapes may be molded. However, the amount of detail depends on the child. At first he will be working with rough forms, and only gradually will he be able to execute finer details.

Below are three different possibilities for fastening additional parts to the basic form.

(1) Prepare a small supply of newspaper strips. Hold the part to be added next to the basic form with one hand, pick up a paper strip covered with paste with the other hand, and stick it over the two parts to be joined.

This has to be repeated several times, in order to cover all the joints where parts are to be attached. These seams have no strength when wet. They will dry in one to three days depending on their thickness.

sufficiently for a strip or stick to be inserted a little way. Following this, the two parts are pasted together with paper strips, as described before. Small balls of paper, pasted on with paper strips in the corners where the two parts meet, will create a smooth transition between the basic form and the added piece. Let the long and slim parts made of paper and paste dry before attaching them to the basic form.

(3) If the paste is used up or put away, it is occasionally necessary to use tape. Work with cellophane tape is quick and clean. Tape, however, presents considerable disadvantages over newspaper and paste: it does not adhere well on an uneven surface, it may not be painted over with watercolors due to its coating, and does not match the background. Once in a while all-purpose glue can be used, particularly where the added piece is not under stress or is small and light.

(2) There is a better method for adding parts that are to protrude farther from the basic form. With a pointed knife, scissors, or an awl, a slot is cut in the basic form where the parts should be attached. If the balloon inside has not yet been removed, it will now be punctured. It will sag and break away from the paper skin with a curious crackling sound. The slot will have to be enlarged

Painting the Surface

With a soft, wide brush, apply an undercoat of white dispersion paint. Dispersion paint, unlike opaque white paint from a paint box, is not water-soluble after it dries. Because of this property, it is suitable as a primer for further painting with water-soluble colors. Wash the brushes with water immediately after use. On top of the white undercoat, watercolors will look brighter if they are mixed with water to a thick paste. When using poster colors or plastic paints, no white undercoat is necessary. The choice of colors should be left entirely to the children. They may prefer realistic coloring (for instance, green for a frog), but this is not necessary. It is their privilege to disregard reality. For children, colors are not just "clothes" for a figure; colors have a symbolic value.

The child's approach to the order of painting details should be as spontaneous and self-assured as his choice of colors. He will tend to paint the obvious characteristics first—such as painting eyes, nose, and mouth before the skin, or the apples on a tree before the green leaves, or the suspenders before the shirt. This complicates further procedures. By demonstrating, for instance, how a person gets dressed ("On top of bare skin comes the shirt, then the sweater, and finally the coat"), it is easy to explain why the undercoat must be applied first. The patterns and details basic to the figure can follow after the primer dries. Not all children will be able to use paints and brushes spontaneously and become inspired without the help of an adult. Certain children will even become inhibited by the multitude of possibilities. They should be encouraged to use simple motifs—such as circles, dots, or lines—suitable for their figure. There are infinite variations of straight lines, which can be applied in waves or clusters. Dots of paint, surrounded by circles in different colors, will stand out or recede according to the choice of colors. Colored circles may be brightened up with one or more dots in a different color in the

center or the margin. Straight lines may continue as waves or zigzag patterns; large circles and dots of color may alternate with small ones. Older children may already realize how to augment the plasticity of a figure by painting large protruding surfaces with large patterns. Receding smaller surfaces will then be painted with a similar but smaller pattern. The eyes, noses, and mouths should al-

ways be brought into relief from the background with contrasting colors or size.

Various Materials for Surface Designs

Various materials may be used instead of painting. Of the many possibilities, a few are listed below:
—tissue paper,
—colored paper,
—aluminum foil,
—fur remnants,
—leather,
—fabric,
—wool,
—string, etc.
If any of these are used, no priming with dispersion color is required.

Tissue paper is stuck on with paste in strips or scraps, and the many creases will create a lively object. (Caution: tissue paper colors run badly when wet, and the spots are hard to remove from clothes.) Obviously tissue paper may also be painted over with watercolors, but if colored scraps and strips are used in the first place, further painting will not be necessary.

Colored paper is heavier than tissue paper and therefore has to be torn or cut in very small pieces in order to prevent creases on a curved surface. The scraps are glued on mosaic-fashion. For a scaly or feathery structure, the scraps are placed in slightly overlapping rows. The color pages of illustrated magazines can also be used. If torn in small pieces and sorted according to basic colors, they will create a multitude of color gradations.

Aluminum foil. If a balloon is covered with aluminum foil, an all-purpose glue must be used. Paste will not dry on foil.

For *fur and leather remnants*, all-purpose glue should also be used. Frequently children will become so fascinated by fur that they will want to cover an entire animal with it. Felt ani-mals are popular because of their softness and plumpness. A balloon covered with fur will only simulate softness, and it would therefore be more sensible to use this material only in small quantities for special effects.

Textiles. A further profusion of uses can be found for wound-up wool, yarn, short pieces of string, fabric strips, and rope. If they are left dangling from a figure, it will look shaggy. Patterns can also be cut from fabrics to make a surface design.

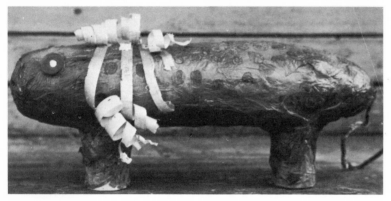

purpose. For such children, it is best to limit the choice. According to the situation, the adult should either hide part of the materials or make a choice himself.

The Final Touches

Once completed, the painted parts of the figure may be covered with a thin layer of lacquer. This is best done with a spray. However, this may produce unhealthy vapors, so it should be done outdoors by an adult.

Decorative Details

The designing of the eyes, nose, and mouth is very important. Also, ears, hair, and a tail may decisively change the entire appearance of a figure. These details may be painted or glued on. For suitable materials there are no limits to the imagination. Here are a few suggestions: wire, corks, sawdust, buttons, branches, cotton, dried beans, dough, bottle caps, rocks, pipe cleaners, wooden spools, corrugated cardboard, feathers, hay, straw, fruit pits, remnants of carpeting, etc.

Selecting from a large collection of materials is great fun for children. There are also children who find it hard to make a decision, and they will keep collecting all kinds of materials. Some children will be distracted quickly and forget their original

Instructions for Specific Figures

Chinese Lanterns Made of Tissue Paper

Cover pieces of tissue paper with paste and stick them directly to the balloon. Since light penetrates this paper well, it will still show through several layers. The fibrous structure and the many tiny creases in the paper, which occur during gluing, thus will become visible. Particularly attractive are layers made with papers of various sizes and colors. Light colors combined with one or two contrasting colors are recommended. Several layers of dark paper on top of each other will soon produce a dark cover that is almost impenetrable by light.

Chinese Lanterns Made of Greaseproof Paper

Like tissue paper, greaseproof paper is glued in scraps directly to the balloon. Combined with paste, this paper will become soft and flexible. Here, too, the same rule applies for colors: light foundation, some dark colors for contrast.

Chinese Lanterns with "Windows"

In the dry, thick-walled basic form, cut out small windows all around and paste larger pieces of tissue paper over them, or paste greaseproof paper on the inside.

Chinese Lanterns Made of Aluminum Foil

With all-purpose glue, stick a layer of foil directly on the balloon. Then cover with the usual number of layers of newspaper. As soon as the form is completely dry, cover with a final layer of aluminum foil, using all-purpose glue. Pierce holes in the sides with various sharp articles, such as a pin, a nail, an awl, etc. Small children may want to make a preliminary pencil sketch.

A Tumbler Doll
A round or pear-shaped balloon
is covered thickly all over with
paper and paste. After the balloon is quite dry, the top third
is cut off in one piece with a
sharp knife. A rock the size of
a fist is covered with all-purpose
glue and placed on the bottom of
the lower part, where it is supported on the sides with small
balls of paper and pasted down
with several strips of paper. This
part may not be moved until it is
completely dry. Finally the top
part is put back on again and
tightly fastened with strips of
paper. Now some other parts
may be added, and the entire
figure can be painted.

Banks
A finished figure becomes a
bank when a slot is cut in the
stomach or back with a pointed
knife. It does not alway have to
be a piggy bank; it can just as
well be a giraffe-bank, a
chicken-bank, a coin-cat, a
penny-elephant, or, as shown
here, a duck-bank.

Half-Balloon Shapes
The example of the ladybug will
demonstrate that half-balloons
present many new design possibilities. Here are some suggestions: a mouse, a hedgehog,
a turtle, a doll buggy, a train,
a car, a cradle, a drum (with a
slot), a mask, etc.

A Rattle

Cover a round balloon right to its tip with a solid layer of paper and let it dry. Then pull the balloon out at the tip to remove it from the stiff form. Now all kinds of noisemaking articles may be dropped through the opening: pebbles, glass splinters, pieces of sheet-metal, wooden balls, etc. Push a wooden stick, about twenty inches long, into the opening and fasten it with paper strips covered with paste. The joint between stick and balloon may be smoothed out with balls of paper and covered with strips of paper. Let the rattle dry in an upright position.

Eggs

If an egg-shaped basic form is cut in half, lengthwise, the result is two halves of an egg whose edges are reinforced with paper strips and paste. A strip of cardboard, about three-fourths-inch wide and measuring the circumference of the egg half, is glued to the inside of one half and hung up to dry with clothespins. Then the egg may be painted and lacquered. If used as a present, it may be filled and decorated with a wide ribbon.

8. BUILDING WITH STYROFOAM

by Herta Petersen

This chapter examines styrofoam for its uses and possibilities as a hobby. Working with styrofoam can involve several different approaches:
(A) Using materials already stamped into certain shapes (for instance, packing materials for electrical equipment). Here the children's reactions will be spontaneous, and they will quickly invent wonderful games with the preshaped parts.

(B) Teaching new techniques to children. With the aid of styrofoam they will quickly and effortlessly become familiar with many mechanical tasks, such as the use of a hammer and nails, or sawing, which can hardly be mastered at this age with any other material. Also, design possibilities, like printing, fusing, painting, building, decorating, are demonstrated.
(C) Assembling objects, such as

ships, houses, or just imaginary creations. Some jobs, like gluing and painting, will come naturally to a child. Of course there will also be some difficulties, and assistance will be needed occasionally.

This chapter explains how the child can be encouraged to experiment with new and unknown materials. Styrofoam offers particularly unlimited, versatile, and inspiring possibilities.

Where to Work

Weather permitting, it is best to work outdoors, or use a rather empty room, which will soon look cheerful due to the material used. Styrofoam crumbles when broken, producing a lot of waste. The snowlike crumbs scatter quickly, but they can be removed easily with a vacuum cleaner.

Properties of the Material

From the outside, styrofoam appears smooth, even shiny. It is, however, a pebbly material of which there are two types, fine and coarse. Styrofoam is rather soft and lightweight. It floats easily and may even carry loads. However, care should be taken that children do not stand on it in deep water without supervision.

Styrofoam is not a hard-wearing plaything. Movable parts cannot be attached to it permanently, so it is eminently suitable for improvisations.

Styrofoam dissolves in all nitrate solutions—turpentine, benzine, lacquers, and color sprays; it skrinks or melts in heat. These properties preclude a number of projects, but at the same time they open up many new possibilities. In the course of working with the material, the children will no doubt develop their own ideas and add new ones.

Where to Buy Styrofoam

Styrofoam is mainly known as packing material for electrical appliances. Frequently one may obtain it free in appliance or hardware stores; they may be only too happy to get rid of surplus waste.

Large slabs and blocks, and thin sheets, which are sold by the foot, may be bought in building-material stores. However, they are not exactly inexpensive. In addition, one can buy very small pieces and balls, which are mostly used for stuffing; also, florists and gardeners may sell pellets that are used for loosening up the soil. Hobby stores carry styrofoam in balls and rings that are used for decorations with straw flowers and similar purposes.

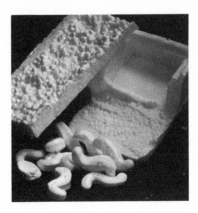

Auxiliary Materials

When building:
—crepe paper,
—florists' wire,
—toothpicks, nails, pins, or
  wooden splinters.
For gluing and fusing:
—all-purpose glue,
—white glue,
—candles.
For painting:
—brushes,
—watercolors or poster paints.
For changing the surface:
—diluted nitrates or turpentine
  and brushes,
—candles.
For decorating:
—buckles, buttons, braids, yarn,
  fabric swatches, brooches,
  paper flowers, thread, scraps
  of wool, screws, feathers, etc.
For printing:
—small roller or brush,
—newspapers, absorbent paper,
  or fabric,
—paint,
—a pane of glass or something
  similar.

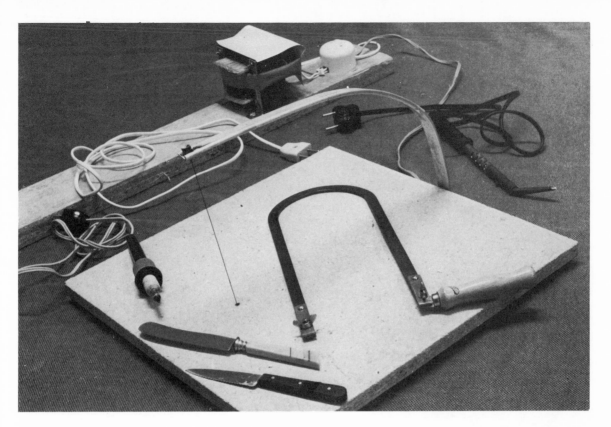

Tools to Use

Obviously, the least dangerous working method is to use your hands for breaking and crumbling. If more precise work is required, styrofoam may be cut with a knife or a fretsaw. An easier method is to cut it with a heated wire. Then there are no crumbs, but it does emit a somewhat disagreeable odor. The same is true of a soldering iron. Of further use are a small hammer, pliers, and scissors.

137

Building with Styrofoam

Even in the raw, styrofoam can have many functions. Sometimes the pieces are so large that they can become rather substantial constructions. Flat pieces become walls, shaped ones represent rooms. The children will imagine castles, motels, hotels (including elevators), garages, and swimming pools in which water may easily be held inside blue-painted hollows.

Pieces with straight edges can be glued together with wide strips of crepe paper. These shapes have many uses: as temporary room decorations, as dividing walls, or as the back walls of a puppet theater.

Another possibility involves interlocking single pieces by carving out corresponding slots with a kitchen knife.

Wood chips, bamboo stems, and pins, the longer the better, are excellent substitutes for nails. They may be hammered in, which is much better than gluing. These nails do not bend, they can be removed easily, and they can be used again and again. Inexpensive florists' wire can also be used for cleaner joints. This may be pushed through the material by hand. If a piece of wire is not pushed in far enough, for example, the styrofoam pieces attached to it swing gaily to and fro. An accident like this produces movement, and it may be an incentive for new ideas. In fact, this is one of the great advantages of the material, since it enables the child to transform his ideas right away. In quick succession he can improvise cars, boats, locomotives, motorcycles, and airplanes. Although they are not durable and cannot be used long for play, they still sustain the children's fascination for many days.

When looking at larger pre-shaped pieces of styrofoam, a child will imagine many different things: a doll house, shops, or stables. A few crosspieces might represent six beds on top of each other, or shelves for merchandise, etc. Sometimes there is already a window opening, requiring only a suitable frame. Additional thought must be put into making styrofoam furniture. However, the many shapes of the material again come in handy: if a piece is cut off in the right place, it makes a straight chair, an armchair, a table. Any missing parts can be glued on.

The shapes of some pieces produce figures by being attached on top of each other or against each other. A contest can be arranged for inventing the best trimmings. For this the children can rummage among odds and ends. This will again produce many new ideas: it is possible to build animals, machines, model trains, and tracks—a multitude of imaginary creations! Some pieces may have a peephole. One child will use this as a mask, another will put the entire piece on his head as a hat. Caution: styrofoam retains heat. After some time, a mask that is too tight may become very warm and sticky.

Gaps between the single pieces, bridged by spikes, may create entirely new images. Wonderful designs may be made with old nails, toothpicks, or old screws. If you are lucky and find feathers, you may invent fancy birds and other whimsical creatures.

143

Painting on Styrofoam

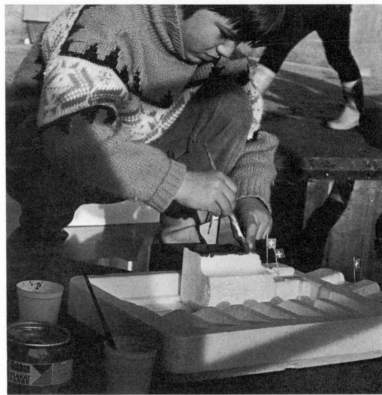

Before the various parts have been painted, constructions may be changed again and again. If paint is used, the design becomes a permanent one, but at the same time its appearance is a lot more cheerful and has the stamp of personality. Since styrofoam is water-repellent, paint will not adhere to it easily, but this problem can be solved with a little soap.

You may also add some soap powder or liquid detergent to the water. The many floating droplets usually show distinctly through the lighter paints. If more luminous colors are preferred, water-soluble poster colors should be used.

Working with a Candle

Styrofoam melts when heated. This property may be utilized when gluing. The surfaces to be joined are held next to a burning candle and then quickly pressed against each other. Children should not do this work alone. They might burn their fingers or become frightened by the flare-up of styrofoam. However, it never really burns, and any flames are easily put out. Therefore there is hardly any real danger, apart from the shock. Nevertheless, an adult should always be close at hand. The flame of the candle can also be used to "paint" black, or to burn off unnecessary corners by holding either the candle to the styrofoam or the styrofoam to the candle. This is a "secret" technique for making masks, for instance, but here again, an adult should be close by in order to help quickly, if necessary.

145

Once the exploring spirit has taken hold, the child will see more and more possibilities of creating something out of even the smallest particles of styrofoam. There are unlimited variations for producing tiny figures. It is a lot of fun to make relief-type pictures attached to a flat piece of styrofoam. For this, the styrofoam stuffing material is very suitable. If glued to a flat surface, it will create a pattern and provide new possibilities for decorating puppets, birds, and trees, among others, and they can then be painted.

Breaking Up Styrofoam

If you need small pieces and only large ones are available, there are several methods for cutting them up. As already mentioned, they may be broken up by hand, cut up with a kitchen knife, or sawn with a fretsaw. In addition, an adult can:
—charge the blade of a fretsaw with low-voltage electricity (about 10 to 20 volts),

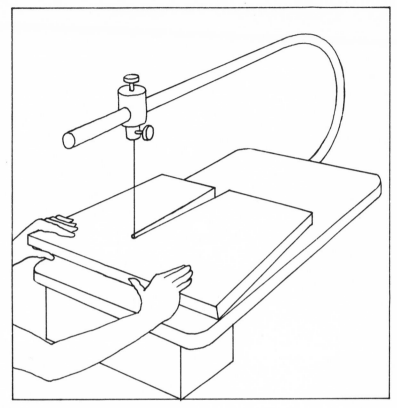

—use a cutting tool with a heated piece of wire,

—use a special styrofoam cutting tool (available in hobby shops),

—use a regular soldering iron, or an electric soldering iron (the latter is not as good, since scraps will stick to it and smolder, producing a bad odor).

With this method, the grown-up may quickly cut out many parts, such as wheels, following the child's instructions. Depending on their experience and dexterity, children may be able to use a saw under supervision. The saw illustrated here was homemade and has a very fine wire, which should not be heated for too long. One child can cut the straight pieces and another one can turn the switch on and off when instructed. An adult should always supervise.

Fusing Structures

Regular or electric soldering irons are very suitable for scratching and drawing. The surface can be painted beforehand, but some children will prefer to paint the scratched-out shapes afterward, and then add further designs. If the child is not very careful, he can quickly burn holes, but this may be fun, and it can be utilized immediately by inserting a piece of colored glass or a marble.

Printing

No other material is quite as suitable for producing printing blocks as styrofoam. The blocks are made from small pieces. Patterns, for instance, may be made by using a nitrate solution, since this will immediately eat into the styrofoam when it is applied with a brush. Here, of course, great caution is required, since this is flammable.

Children should not inhale the vapors, which are harmful to the lungs. However, a soldering iron is also a suitable tool for making patterns, but it produces a more mechanical design. The burnt parts do not discolor; they only smell during the work. A pointed instrument or a nail is also good for scratching. Once the stamping is completed, the block can be painted. Paint is mixed with a roller on a nonabsorbent surface (such as a pane of glass), and it is applied thoroughly to the block. Then the block is pressed firmly against the surface on which the printing is to be done and carefully lifted off.

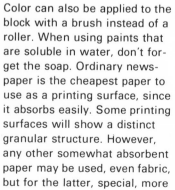

Color can also be applied to the block with a brush instead of a roller. When using paints that are soluble in water, don't forget the soap. Ordinary newspaper is the cheapest paper to use as a printing surface, since it absorbs easily. Some printing surfaces will show a distinct granular structure. However, any other somewhat absorbent paper may be used, even fabric, but for the latter, special, more expensive colors are needed. Since the color on the block will dry after printing, a different color may be used for each new printing. Once in a while, the block may be washed under running water. The amount of color needed and the most suitable size block for a particular child can only be determined during the course of the work.

What has been said up to now will indicate that styrofoam may be used not only to occupy a single child, but it is particularly suitable for cooperative work. It is a waste product and inexpensive. It may already be used as a toy in itself without any additions, but the child may also experiment by combining many things, such as color or wire, or by practicing an ancient technique of printing. Styrofoam is easy to handle and thus encourages spontaneous inspiration, and it provides ever-changing games for children. Even the "snow" that results from the work provides extra fun, so that children deliberately produce even more of it. It is not surprising that children are using a new substance, such as styrofoam, more freely and are more ready to experiment than the adult who frequently rejects this material as too artificial and unpleasant to the touch and therefore does not regard it as an acceptable toy.

9. MOLDING AND MODELING

by Isolde Schmitt-Menzel

This chapter shows how children can learn to use modeling materials in a playful way. An adult should not let children copy completed models; he should just give simple instructions. Plastic figures are made from basic forms, such as spheres, cubes, or cylinders. This creative activity will develop a child's imagination, strengthen his self-assurance, and develop his feeling for form and space.

The most important tools for molding and modeling are the hands. Other requirements are a wooden or fiber board, a kitchen knife for cutting, a pencil for making indentations, and an empty beer bottle for rolling. The molding material should be neither sticky (too moist) nor hard (too dry). The most suitable molding material is clay. If wrapped in a damp cloth and a plastic bag, this clay can be used for many months. Additional molding materials are:

Clayola. This material may be molded again and again without hardening. It is obtainable in all colors.

Art Utility moist pottery clay is a material for molding; it hardens without baking in a kiln. It can be painted after drying.

Sculpey stays soft indefinitely or bakes hard in a kitchen stove. It is suitable for young children.

Mexican pottery clay can be air-dried to a rich red color. It becomes quite hard and can be painted.

Amaco modeling dough is soft and pliable. It will not stick to hands, furniture, or clothing. It may be painted.

All the materials mentioned, or similar products, may be purchased in hobby shops, hobby departments of department stores, or paint shops.

To begin working, tear small pieces from a large lump of clay and shape them into balls with your hands flat. If you stick a nail in the still-moist ball and thread a piece of string through the hole after the ball dries, you will have a necklace. Large pieces of clay should be rolled into balls on the table. If you press small balls firmly on top of a large one, you will have a tree. Several large balls make a snowman. If you let the children combine balls of many sizes, they will be delighted with the results: round animals, flowers, human figures. If you press a large sphere firmly on the table, you will obtain a hemisphere, and if you poke holes in it, you will have a holder for brushes, flowers, or pencils. But you can also create hedgehogs, the sun, or a face, just by adding more pieces. Children should be shown that even the more complicated figures begin with simple basic shapes. All the forms should be attached accurately and firmly.

153

154

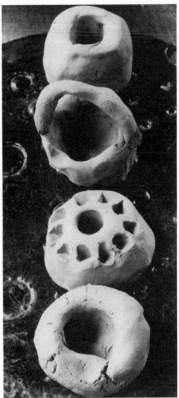

The pieces for a game board shown here were made by combining two spheres. The eyes and mouth are marked with a pencil; the nose is a tiny sphere. To make pieces for Chinese checkers, cut quarter-inch slices off a roll of clay. These activities are simple enough for even the smallest children to enjoy. Particular favorites are sandwiches, breads, cakes, and sausages for filling a play food market. A hole pressed into a sphere, for instance, will make a small candlestick; if this hole is enlarged, the object becomes a small cup; a roll of clay attached to each side makes a basket for shopping.

Next, shape a roll of clay. There are unlimited possibilities for creating figures: snails, flowers, stars, or the sun. Let these rather fragile pieces dry on the work table. Particular attention should be paid to firming the joints between the individual

parts. Quarter-inch slices are shown here being cut from a roll. They can be painted in different colors or decorated with patterns, and also used as pieces for Chinese checkers

or chess men. Make a tree with one thick roll and many thinner ones. The branches should be pressed on very firmly. Leaves and fruit may be added. Thin rolls may also be made into wheels, pretzels, snakes, numerals, and letters.

157

The crocodile shown here was made out of a long roll of clay. The legs were shaped from four small rolls, the feet flattened out. The eyes were made of small balls of clay and the mouth was cut open with a knife.

In a thick roll of clay, press a hole with a brush or the handle of a spoon. Hold the brush with your right hand and roll the piece of clay backward and forward with your left hand. The result is a pitcher or a vase.

If you want to make a proper clay container, single rolls of clay should be placed on top of each other, as the girl is doing in the picture shown here. Many thin rolls, one after another, are firmly pressed on top of each other. The pot with the handle and the funny little woman were also made with rolls. Later on, when she is dry and has been painted, a candle will be inserted in her hat.

Now the clay is rolled flat with an old rolling pin. This can also be done with an empty bottle. It is best for small children to kneel on a chair when "rolling out the dough." Before it is rolled out, the lump of clay should be beaten flat with both fists. This exercise is fun for children. As a rule, their concentration on a particular creation tends to be interrupted by the urge for motion, whether it is beating, kneading, or pounding the clay. Adults should refrain from criticizing an unfinished piece that a child regards as completed. The child does the best he can. If he feels it is not good enough, he will lose his enjoyment, patience, and self-confidence.

With a knife, the fish, mask, cat, owl, mouse, and man are cut out of the flatly rolled clay. As needed, thin or thick rolls, balls of clay representing eyes, noses, heads, fins, feathers, etc., are attached to these figures.

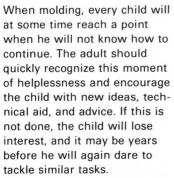

When molding, every child will at some time reach a point when he will not know how to continue. The adult should quickly recognize this moment of helplessness and encourage the child with new ideas, technical aid, and advice. If this is not done, the child will lose interest, and it may be years before he will again dare to tackle similar tasks.

The turtle shown here was made from a hemisphere (by knocking a sphere on the table) and three rolls of clay pressed underneath as legs, head, and tail.

163

The two piggy banks are made as follows: cut a thick roll or sphere in half and make a hollow in each half. Then press the two halves together carefully, and smooth over the joint. Small rolls are used for nose, ears, and legs. Cut a slot in the back for the money. The basic shapes from which the other figures have been made are easily recognizable. For instance, the wings of the penguins are two flat-tened rolls. The hair of the small seated man was made of very thin rolls.

The cat was made by an older child. The single parts are well attached to each other and the joints are smoothed over with clay. If you want to make a cube, flatten the sides of a clay sphere with a small wooden board.

The edges of dice should be slightly rounded for easier rolling. The intriguing city shown here was built of large and small cubes. The windows, doors, and gates were impressed with a pencil, the back of a brush, and a clothespin. If you are working with a group, you may want to consider this or a similar theme in advance. Try, for example, a village, a zoo, a store, a doll house, or a Christmas creche. These suggestions will help the children overcome their initial shyness or indecision, and the common goal will stimulate them. Each should be assigned a special small task, so even the weaker children will feel like equals by being able to contribute to the group work.

What materials are best for models?

Clay. This is ideal for kneading and is suitable for all models. Children's hands can easily shape this material. Unfortunately, clay has the disadvantage of not hardening without being fired in a ceramic kiln. After the first firing in the oven, the piece will have to be glazed and then fired again. Therefore, if you are working with clay, it is advisable to locate a kiln that can be used for firing.

Sculpey is soft and may therefor be used by the child for a variety of shapes.

Plaster of paris. This is best for making pure white castings or molds.

Plasticine is nonhardening and nontoxic and comes in many colors.

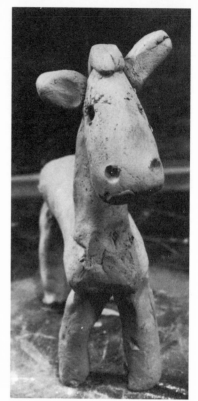

Here is a potter's workshop. Youth hostels, schools, and adult-education classes sometimes have such workshops. The bowls, pots, dishes, and vases in the front have already been baked once; next they will be glazed. In order to bake such clay models, you will need an electric oven that can reach temperatures of 1620° Fahrenheit to 1980° Fahrenheit.

10. KITES

by Elisabeth Gloor

The construction of kites makes great demands on childrens' perseverance, determination, and dexterity. Most parts of the operation can be done by the child unaided, but others require adult help. The construction of kites is suitable for five-year-old children, but there are enough possibilities that younger ones can participate in the project. Children will enjoy working in small groups when they can help each other, thus gaining a feeling of independence. If possible, the work should be extended over two or three half-days.

Obviously, kites may also be bought ready-made. This would eliminate the search for materials and the time it takes for construction. The child would not have to handle any tools, and there would be no risk of failure when the kite is flown. However, one thus deprives the child of an important opportunity to construct and create. The construction of kites also contributes to the experience of learning all the rules and conditions necessary for successful flying. The child will be provided with a basis for understanding certain laws of physics in a non-scientific context. Only if a child has participated in the entire working process will he be able to repair a kite or design other types of kites. He will become familiar with the subject and thus be capable of original inventions and truly creative activities.

Ready-made kites obviously are capable of flying, as much as ready-made trains and cars will move, or all technical toys will function. A home-made kite will also fly, because the child has built it well and has learned to consider the conditions necessary for flying. The ultimate success will therefore be a hard-earned achievement and the outcome of a resolute effort. For the child, this will be a rewarding experience of a job well done.

Materials Needed

Wooden strips, nails, twine, paper or plastic sheets, four small hooks, size or all-purpose glue.

Tools Needed

Hammer, saw, scissors, tape measure, ruler, felt pens. For decoration you may use: wax crayons, poster paints and brushes, finger paints, broad felt-tip pens, colored paper, paste, self-adhesive foil.

Size of Kite

The larger the surface facing the wind, the better the kite will fly, but more strength will be required of the child to make it rise. Therefore, the kite should not be longer than the height of the child. A larger kite requires more materials, which will make it more substantial and therefore increase its total weight. For the sake of buoyancy, the kite should be as light as possible. The pointed kite described here should have a minimum length of two feet, since a smaller surface would make its flight unstable. The maximum length for the kite is four feet. For larger kites there are other, more suitable designs.

Wooden Strips

Wooden strips suitable for the frame of a kite frequently may be found around the house. They also may be bought in hobby shops or ordered from a lumber yard. It is essential that they be of light wood (fir, pine) with the grain running lengthwise, dry, and free of knots. The ratio of the lengthwise and the crosswise strips should be about 3:2 (for instance, 24 inches:16 inches). The ratio of the length to the width should be approximately 2:1, 3:1, or 3:2. The longer the wooden strip, the stronger it should be. For a small kite, strips of about four inches by one-eighth inch are sufficient; for larger kites, about eight inches by one-fourth inch. Measurements for a medium-sized kite would be: lengthwise strip, thirty inches; crosswise strip, twenty inches; size of strip, four inches by one-fourth inch.

Covering Materials

You may use kite paper, colored parchment, greaseproof paper, or lightweight paper with a smooth laminated surface. Each material has its advantages and disadvantages as to breaking strength, weight, transparency, or water repel-lency. Brown wrapping paper, which was used frequently in the past, is not recommended, since it is comparatively heavy and may have only one laminated side. There are unlimited possibilities for experimenting with new materials, such as plastics (shopping bags and garbage bags).

Twine

You may be able to obtain special twine for kites in stationery shops. This twine is already wound on rolls or spools, but these spools are usually too small for children to handle, since their hands may be too clumsy. Smaller children, in particular, should use stronger and more substantial materials. A fine line made of hemp may also be used. This is heavier than the usual kite twine, and in order to obtain the required length of 200 yards, several balls will have to be tied together. Both kite twine and hemp are inexpensive, but they do have the disadvantage of becoming wet and heavy in the grass. Nylon line, similar to the kind used for fishing, does not absorb moisture; it is lightweight, but it is also very expensive and hard to disentangle.

The Tail and Ears of the Kite

For the tail and tassels, cut strips of colored paper remnants. Suitable materials are tissue paper, crepe paper, toilet paper, newspaper. If you have to buy it, purchase two rolls of tissue paper or crepe paper in various colors. To sum up: a kite has to be light in weight and stable; the largest possible surface a child can handle should be facing the wind.

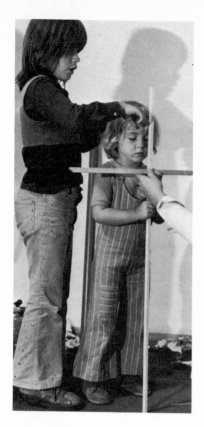

Construction

This requires a lot of space. Cover one corner of the room with newspaper, large pieces of cardboard, or opened-up brown paper bags. Children enjoy using the floor as a working surface. There should be a minimum area of ten square feet per child. Keep a chair ready as a prop for sawing.

Wooden strips ordered from a lumber yard will already be cut to exact sizes. Any others will have to be sawn to the correct measurements. The desired length of the wooden strip is marked with a pencil line. For sawing, the strip is placed on the chair with the mark very close to the chair's surface; the part to be cut off is unsupported. The child should hold down the strip with his left knee and left

hand. His thumb should be placed to the left of the mark. Then he should make a small incision along the line by sliding the saw across it several times. Now the saw can grip the wood, and he can saw carefully to and fro. This job requires some practice, but it is a lot of fun for older children. The hands of three-to-six-year-old children should be guided.

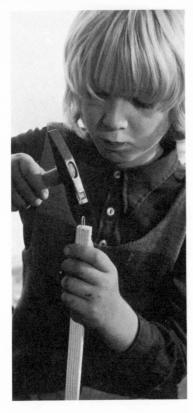

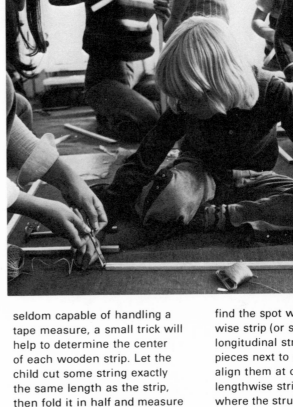

Children can help each other when hammering the hooks into the ends of the wooden strips. One child can hold the strip, the other can hammer. Hammering requires great security and coordination of both hands. For some children it may help if a grown-up first hammers the hooks lightly into the wood. Leave a sufficiently large loop so that two strands can be pulled through. Since children are seldom capable of handling a tape measure, a small trick will help to determine the center of each wooden strip. Let the child cut some string exactly the same length as the strip, then fold it in half and measure with this folded string from one end of the strip to the center, where he can make a mark. To find the spot where the crosswise strip (or strut) crosses the longitudinal strip, place both pieces next to each other and align them at one end. On the lengthwise strip, mark the spot where the strut terminates. The grown-up should check this with a tape measure, since it is essential for the proper balance of the kite that all measurements be marked correctly. Then the wooden strips are placed at

 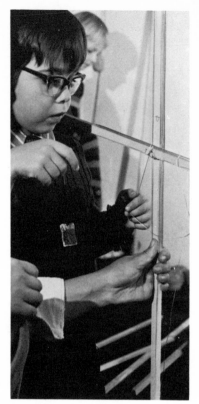 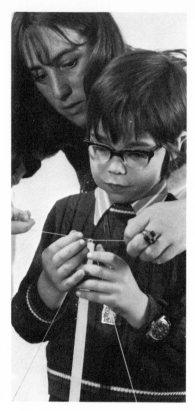

right angles to each other—
with the two marks exactly
matching—and tacked down
with a thin nail whose point
has been blunted by a slight
tap with a hammer. This will
prevent the wood from splitting.

If the pieces are attached
loosely, they can no longer
slip sideways. Reinforce this
connection with string as follows: one child should hold the
longitudinal strip, while another
child slides a loop of string over
one end of the strip and ties up
the strips like cross-stitch in
needlework. The string should
be stretched very tightly and
then knotted at the end. If the

cross is lopsided, this can be
corrected later.
Now the child can thread some
string through all the hooks,
starting at the tail end and going
from there to one side, then to
the top, back to the other side,
and then to the tail, where
the two ends should be pulled
tight and knotted by an adult.
Now adjust the framework by
placing the two wooden strips

exactly at right angles to each other. Cover the ends of the strips with some glue, so that the string can no longer slip out of place.

Next spread the covering paper flat on the floor and place the wooden framework on top of it. One child traces the outline of the string with a felt pen with- out touching it, while another child holds it down. Add another two to four inches on each side. This is best done by placing a ruler against the already exist- ing line and drawing another line outside of it. The second line will be the cutting line.

Decorating the kite presents the first chance for the children to use their creative abilities freely. They should be reminded that the kite will ultimately float high in the air, so in order to have recognizable eyes, teeth, or nose, these features have to be sufficiently large. On parchment one can use paint or paste, on plastics one can draw with wide felt-tip pens, on grease-proof or kite paper one can use either felt pens or wax crayons. Since kite paper is transparent, it is particularly attractive with leftover pieces of similar or varying colors pasted on top of each other. Similar colors on top of each other will make it darker, while different colors will create new hues. Blue and yellow will become green, red and green will become brown, red and blue will become violet. If you have no leftover pieces of transparent paper, you can buy a pad of multicolored transparent sheets in any stationery store.

Children with unsteady hands may find it easier to use plates, cups, or plastic containers for drawing circles, which they can then cut out and paste on. When poster colors are used, an adult should make sure that they are not mixed with too much water Since wet paper tears easily, it has to be completely dry before the next operation is started.

Next the framework will have to be covered. Cut the paper off to about three-eighths inch from the wood at the ends of the crossed strips, or roll it to the same distance. These corners are most vulnerable and may tear later. If the paper has been torn, it should be strengthened with cellophane tape.

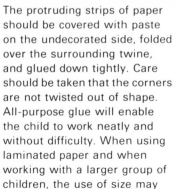

The protruding strips of paper should be covered with paste on the undecorated side, folded over the surrounding twine, and glued down tightly. Care should be taken that the corners are not twisted out of shape. All-purpose glue will enable the child to work neatly and without difficulty. When using laminated paper and when working with a larger group of children, the use of size may

have advantages: it saturates the paper, makes it more pliable and easier to handle, and tautens it again after drying. Larger quantities may be prepared according to instructions on the package.

The children may want to attach tassels at each end of the cross-wise wooden strip. Suitable materials for tassels are tissue paper, crepe paper, napkins, colored newspaper, or toilet paper.

Cut deep notches about one inch apart along the sides of two four-inch-by-eight-inch strips of paper, then roll them up and tie them together tightly with a piece of string as long as the kite. These tassels are knotted to the hooks, leaving the longer ends of string hanging temporarily; they will be used later for balancing.

At the top of the kite, attach a piece of string the same length as the ones on the sides. Attach a string double this length at the tail end, knotting it to the hook with one end longer than the other. The short end will be used later on for stabilizing the tail, the long one for balancing. After all the pieces of string are in place, four hooks may be hammered tightly into the wood.

Now the kite should be placed on the floor, face up; the corner strings are then knotted together. This balancing is the most delicate job of all kite constructing and should be done by an adult. For the center knot to be in the correct position, it has to be about twenty inches from the frame, and it should be at exactly right angles to the intersection of the wooden strips. If the kite is suspended freely from this knot, its top should be higher than its tail, and the two sides should hang at exactly the same level. Inaccurate balancing may seriously impair the kite's ability to fly:

—if the knot is not placed exactly above the center rib, the flight may be lopsided;

—if the knot is made too close to the front, the kite will float almost horizontally, and it will topple over as soon as it is not being pulled;

—if the knot is made too close to the back, the kite will float in too much of an upright position. Since this would prevent it from sailing on an air cushion, it would crash.

The tail is attached only after the kite has been balanced. It is a string four times the length of the kite and may be decorated with colored strips of paper, six inches apart. Use the same kind of paper as used for the tassels, which may be either folded like a

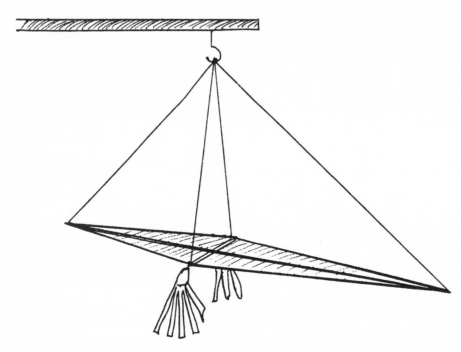

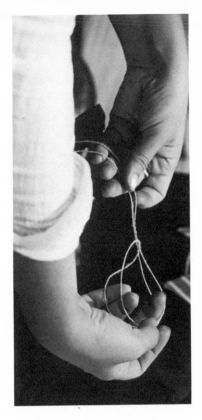

fan or cut in three-quarter-inch-
wide strips. These are gathered
in a bundle and fastened by
loops of string (see illustration).
Tie another tassel to the end of
the tail. This is cut the same
way as the ones for the sides,
but it is larger. The finished tail
is attached to the frame with a
short piece of string hanging
at the bottom end of the kite.

The only thing left is to find a spool for winding the twine. There are the following possibilities:
—the spool may be cut out of cardboard, about four inches by

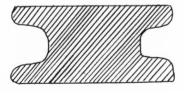

eight inches (see illustration);
—use an empty string spool, like those used in stores for packing;
—stick an old piece of wood in the ground in order to watch the kite during calm weather; or
—cut a piece from a broom, about twelve inches long, and glue and nail round cardboard disks to each end.
Now wind the long twine over this spool. In order to avoid tangling, do this in the shape

of a figure eight, as shown in the photograph. Tie the end of the twine to the knot in the center of the kite, which is used for balancing, and now it is ready to fly.

How to Make the Kite Fly

Building a kite is quite an achievement for the small builder. It taxes his exactness, his imagination, his ability to build according to instructions, and his perseverance. Once these hurdles have been overcome, the moment of flying is eagerly awaited. It may then be a great disappointment for the child if the kite is finished on a rainy or calm day. Even the most beautiful, light, and carefully constructed kite will not fly without wind. For flying the kite you will also have to find a large meadow without rocks and rubble, which impede running and may tear the paper. Further, it should be far away from trees (which catch the tails of kites), and away from high-tension wires and television antennas, which may come in contact with the kite and be dangerous for children. Another danger is proximity to an airport.

Once the proper meadow has been found, the exact direction of the wind has to be determined. This is done by holding in the air a piece of thread or a wet finger, or by throwing a ball of tissue paper straight up in the air. The last method is rather difficult for children. Next, two people should stand one behind the other, against the direction of the wind, about thirty yards apart. The person in the back places the tail of the kite on the ground and, while gripping the frame, holds it up vertically. The person in front holds the spool. The twine between them is tightened. On an agreed-upon sign, the person in front starts to run against the wind, at the same time, the person in back releases the kite with a slight push. If the kite rises immediately and the twine remains taut, more twine may be unwound while the kite flyer runs. If the kite does not have enough power to rise after several trials, the tail may have to be shortened by about one yard. However, the last tassel has to be attached again at the end.

To start a kite flying is an extremely difficult task for children of three to five, since their entire attention is concentrated on their own locomotion. This is the time when an adult should help. If there is enough wind, the twine may be unwound entirely, and no more running will be necessary. After that the child may take over again. Children of six to eight years may be able to do it all on their own. With a twine of 200 yards and wind pressure from the side, the height of the flight will be reduced by more than half of the length of twine. If you have reached the end of the twine, and the kite can still fly higher, the twine may be lengthened by adding more twine, which should be prepared in advance. It is very seldom that a kite will remain floating calmly in the air; therefore it should be watched constantly. If it loses height, the twine should be pulled in for a few yards without being rewound. This will make the kite face the wind in a more upright position, and it will rise again. Soon afterward it will again start to drop, and more action will be required.

This produces continual changes: rising and falling of the kite, pulling and releasing of the twine. In time the child will feel when and how much of the twine to release, and he may therefore give up watching. One of the most fascinating aspects of kite flying, an activity enjoyed by both children and adults, is that one can never anticipate what the kite is going to do next, but one can learn to feel and to react correctly to each variation of the wind pressure.

INDEX